Betty Crocker's
All-Time Favorites

 **GOLDEN PRESS · NEW YORK**
Western Publishing Company, Inc.
Racine, Wisconsin

Photography Director: LEN WEISS

Ninth Printing, 1978

Contents

All-Time Favorites . . .

If anything could please us more than the recipes in this collection, it's the number of good friends we've made through the years. There are the hundreds of Betty Crocker home economists, past and present, who develop and perfect our recipes. The home testers who double-check them. And you, of course—the women who use our recipes day after day, year after year, and take the time to let us know how you like them. Only with the help of all these friends were we able to bring you this, our personal collection of all-time favorite recipes.

You might say that work on this book began in the 1920's, when some of these recipes, like Oatmeal Bread and Corn Pudding, were developed. It was back in those days, too, that we initiated our kitchen testing program. Later, kitchen testing was supplemented by home testing, ensuring the famous "Betty Crocker difference"—the knowledge that if you follow the recipes exactly, you can be sure of perfect results.

The photo from our scrapbook shows some of the first Betty Crocker home economists at work. (Note the test kitchen—ultramodern by 1920 standards.) Then, as now, they would alter and adjust, check and recheck to make sure every recipe was not only as delicous as it could be, but as "mistake-proof," too. If the recipe passed their rigid tests, it was ready for the next crucial step—on-the-spot testing in a homemaker's kitchen. Then the home testers reported back on the availability of ingredients, the clarity of directions and, perhaps most important, the reactions of their families.

The first official Betty Crocker "portrait" —1936.

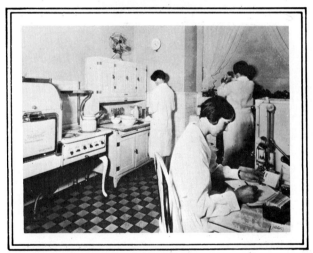

Our first test kitchen.

Recipe cards—from the Cooking School of the Air.

*Recipes via the radio—
thanks to our
Cooking School of the Air.*

*A collection of
our early recipe pamphlets . . .
and our first cookbook.*

Now, how did we first go about sharing these kitchen-tested recipes with you? Back in the 20's, radio was the obvious way, so we launched our Cooking School of the Air. The recipes were slowly dictated to listeners—and we also passed along tips for meal planning and shopping. Thousands of women all over the country enrolled in the school and learned to rely on Betty Crocker recipes. Many began to collect the charming recipe cards (see the preceding page) which were offered to members of the school. By that time, we were also putting the recipes in pamphlets and booklets.

But times were changing—and our recipes changed, too. During the Depression, for instance, low-cost ingredients were important, and we stressed budget-minded recipes. During World War II, rationing was the challenge, and we concentrated on recipes and menus that cut down on butter, meats and sugar. We spread the word in a special booklet called *Your Nation's Rations*.

New ingredients and new kitchen equipment influenced our recipe development, too. Thanks to hydrogenated shortening and the electric mixer we were able to develop a one-bowl method for making cakes. And in 1948, we introduced the "first really new cake in 100 years"—the light and airy chiffon. Its secret ingredient? Salad oil!

Changing interests were another factor that affected the types of recipes we created. In the years that followed World War II, world-traveling Americans wanted recipes for polenta and pilau, for tamale pie and lamb curry. We featured international recipes on our network television program. They were also included in our first best-seller—the original *Betty Crocker's Picture Cook Book*, published in 1950.

In the 50's and 60's, women began to spend more and more time outside the home—pursuing careers, continuing their education, involving themselves in community activities. Because of this, we began to focus more of our kitchen testing on speedier, easier meal planning. Mixes and convenience foods were developed, and it was then that Mocha Brownie Torte and Velvet Crumb Cake were added to our ever-expanding recipe collection. As we constantly streamlined methods and looked to the future with new ideas, more and more hands were needed—until now it takes a staff of about 60 women to do the work of Betty Crocker.

Today we do our kitchen testing in seven colorful, modern kitchens, which thousands of visitors tour each year. Here we still analyze the reports of the home testers, now 1,300 strong throughout the country. Here we answer an average of 3,000 letters and 2,000 phone calls each month. And here, of course, we also compile our cookbooks. To keep in touch with current needs and interests, from time to time we have face-to-face conversations with women in all parts of the United States —and we call these get-togethers our Betty Crocker "pipeline."

These, then, are just some of the activities and influences that have helped us create and develop, select and perfect 12,000 recipes in the course of years—a collection we like to think of as America's best recipes. Thus the task of choosing the ones for this book was by no means an easy one. But thanks to what thousands of homemakers and our own home economists have told us over the years, we made our selections. We hope you'll find many of your own all-time favorites on the pages that follow.

Today's Betty Crocker "portrait."

*One of our seven
modern test kitchens.*

Meats and Main Dishes

Meats and Main Dishes

What makes a main dish something to remember? What makes it a recipe you come back to—time and time again? Not taste alone, you tell us. Built-in cooking secrets count, too. (And who doesn't like to share a secret or two?) Like...what's the easiest way to fry chicken? In the oven, where there's no splattering, no need to watch. What can you do with a pork roast to make sure it will be moist and tender? Roast it in foil—and it practically makes its own gravy. Do you think dumplings are tricky? Our method is based on a simple two-step steaming tip: uncovered to begin with, then covered. They're light as a cloud, every time.

Do-ahead tips make a recipe memorable, too. You tell us that you like main dishes that can be put together one day and popped into the oven the next. Cheese Strata and Chicken-Wild Rice Casserole fill that category deliciously, and are perfect solutions to a busy schedule of errands, meetings, work—or maybe all three. For do-in-advance dinner parties, rely on Hamburger Stroganoff or the classic Burgundy Beef. Either one can be prepared *and* cooked the day before, then reheated.

Of course, we know intriguing and unusual flavor combinations can make a recipe famous. Two such stars are Pork Chops Supreme and Avery Island Deviled Shrimp. They're among the special favorites we serve to our own guests in the Betty Crocker dining room. Creole Flounder's a colorful choice, too. Perfect for the calorie conscious.

These, then, are just some of the tips we've shared with you through the years. You'll find others throughout this chapter, woven neatly into the recipes. We'd love to know which become your secrets to success.

On the preceding pages:
Avery Island Deviled Shrimp,
Burgundy Beef,
Chicken-Sausage Pies,
Pork Roast with Onion Gravy

ROUND STEAK ROYALE

1½- to 2-pound beef round steak
    (top or bottom) or
    tip steak, ¾ inch thick
  ½ cup all-purpose flour*
  1 teaspoon salt
  1 teaspoon paprika
  ¼ teaspoon pepper
  ¼ cup shortening
  1 can (4 ounces) mushroom stems
    and pieces, drained (reserve
    liquid)
  1 large onion, sliced
  ½ cup dairy sour cream
  ¼ cup water

*If using self-rising flour, decrease salt to ½ teaspoon.

Cut the meat into 4 to 6 serving pieces. Mix flour, salt, paprika and pepper; coat meat with the flour mixture. Melt shortening in a large skillet and brown meat over medium heat, 15 to 20 minutes. (If you like a rich, brown gravy, be sure to brown the meat slowly and thoroughly.)

Add enough water to the reserved mushroom liquid to measure ½ cup; pour into the skillet. Top meat with onion slices and mushrooms. Cover tightly and simmer until tender, 1½ to 2 hours, adding a little water if necessary.

Remove the meat to a warm platter. To make the gravy, stir sour cream and ¼ cup water into the skillet and heat *just* to boiling, stirring constantly.

4 TO 6 SERVINGS.

ROUND STEAK WITH RICH GRAVY

3 pounds beef round steak (top
    or bottom) or tip steak,
    1 inch thick
⅓ cup all-purpose flour
3 tablespoons shortening
1 envelope (about 1½ ounces)
    onion soup mix
½ cup water
1 can (10¾ ounces) condensed
    cream of mushroom soup

Sprinkle one side of the meat with half the flour and pound in. (Use a mallet or the edge of a heavy saucer.) Turn meat and pound in the remaining flour. Cut into 6 to 8 serving pieces.

Melt shortening in a large skillet and brown meat slowly and thoroughly over medium heat, 15 to 20 minutes. Sprinkle onion soup mix over meat. Mix water and mushroom soup and pour over meat. Cover tightly and simmer until tender, 1½ to 2 hours, adding a little water if necessary.

Remove the meat to a warm platter. Heat the remaining gravy mixture to boiling, stirring constantly, and pour over the meat.

6 TO 8 SERVINGS.

BURGUNDY BEEF

3½ to 4 pounds beef round steak (top or bottom) or tip steak, 1 inch thick
¼ cup shortening or bacon drippings
5 large onions, sliced
1 pound fresh mushrooms, sliced
3 tablespoons flour
2 teaspoons salt
¼ teaspoon marjoram
¼ teaspoon thyme
¼ teaspoon pepper
1 cup beef bouillon*
2 cups red Burgundy

*Beef bouillon can be made by dissolving 1 beef bouillon cube or 1 teaspoon instant beef bouillon in 1 cup boiling water, or use canned beef broth.

Cut the meat into 1-inch cubes. Melt shortening in a Dutch oven and brown meat, about a third at a time, over medium heat. Remove meat and set aside.

Cook and stir onion and mushrooms in the Dutch oven until onion is tender, adding more shortening if necessary. Remove vegetables and set aside.

Return meat to the Dutch oven and sprinkle with flour and seasonings. Stir in bouillon and wine and heat to boiling. Lower the heat just enough to keep the mixture simmering. Cover and simmer until meat is tender, about 1¼ hours. Check once in a while to see that the liquid just covers the meat. If necessary, add more bouillon and wine (1 part bouillon to 2 parts wine). Add mushrooms and onion to the meat and heat through, stirring occasionally.

8 SERVINGS.

OVEN-BARBECUED ROUND STEAK

3 pounds beef round steak (top or bottom) or tip steak, ¾ inch thick
2 tablespoons salad oil
½ cup chopped onion
¾ cup catsup
½ cup vinegar
¾ cup water
1 tablespoon brown sugar
1 tablespoon prepared mustard
1 tablespoon Worcestershire sauce
½ teaspoon salt
⅛ teaspoon pepper

Cut the meat into 6 to 8 serving pieces. Heat oil in a large skillet and brown meat over medium heat, 15 to 20 minutes. Transfer the meat to an ungreased casserole. (You don't have to do this if your skillet is ovenproof.)

Mix the remaining ingredients and pour over the meat. Cover and cook in 325° oven until tender, 1½ to 2 hours.

6 TO 8 SERVINGS.

CHINESE BEEF AND PEA PODS

1-pound beef tenderloin or boneless
   sirloin steak, ¾ inch thick
1 tablespoon soy sauce
1 thin slice fresh gingerroot,
   crushed*
1 clove garlic, crushed*
1 package (7 ounces) frozen
   Chinese snow peas
¼ cup salad oil
¼ pound fresh mushrooms, sliced
3 stalks Chinese cabbage, cut
   diagonally into ¼-inch slices
   (about 2 cups)
1 medium onion, sliced
½ can (8-ounce size) water chestnuts,
   drained and thinly sliced
1 can (5 ounces) bamboo shoots,
   drained
1 can (13¾ ounces) chicken broth
   (1⅔ cups)
3 tablespoons cornstarch
2 tablespoons soy sauce
½ teaspoon salt
¼ teaspoon sugar
   Chow mein noodles or
   hot cooked rice

*Place gingerroot and garlic between two pieces of
waxed paper and crush with a wooden mallet.

Cut the meat across the grain into very thin slices. (You'll find it much easier to slice the meat if it's partially frozen—or ask your meatman to slice it for you.) Mix 1 tablespoon soy sauce, the gingerroot and garlic and sprinkle on meat; toss until meat is coated. For extra flavor, let marinate at least 30 minutes.

Place frozen snow peas in a colander or sieve and run cold water over pods just until they're separated. Drain.

Heat 2 tablespoons of the salad oil in a large skillet and brown meat over medium-high heat, turning once. Remove meat to a warm platter.

Add the remaining 2 tablespoons salad oil to the skillet and cook and stir mushrooms, cabbage, onion, water chestnuts and bamboo shoots over high heat 2 minutes. Stir in snow peas and 1 cup of the chicken broth. Cover and cook over medium heat 2 minutes.

Mix remaining chicken broth, the cornstarch, soy sauce, salt and sugar and pour into the skillet. Cook, stirring constantly, until the mixture thickens and boils. Boil and stir 1 minute. Add the meat and heat through. Serve over chow mein noodles.

4 SERVINGS.

DILLED POT ROAST

2 tablespoons flour
1 teaspoon salt
¼ teaspoon pepper
3-pound beef chuck pot roast (arm or blade)
1 tablespoon shortening
¼ cup water
1 tablespoon vinegar
1 teaspoon dill weed
6 small potatoes, pared
6 carrots, quartered
½ teaspoon salt
4 or 5 zucchini (about 1 pound), quartered
½ teaspoon salt
Sour Cream Gravy (below)

Mix flour, 1 teaspoon salt and the pepper and rub on the meat. Melt shortening in a large skillet or Dutch oven and brown meat over medium heat. (For a rich, brown gravy, brown the meat slowly and thoroughly.)

Drain off fat and add water and vinegar. Sprinkle half the dill weed on meat; turn and sprinkle with the remaining dill weed. Cover and simmer until tender, 2½ to 3 hours, adding a little water if necessary.

About 1 hour before the end of the cooking time, add potatoes and carrots and sprinkle with ½ teaspoon salt. Cover and simmer 40 minutes.

Add zucchini and sprinkle with ½ teaspoon salt. Cover and simmer 20 minutes longer or until the vegetables are tender. Remove the meat and vegetables to a platter and keep warm while making Sour Cream Gravy.

4 TO 6 SERVINGS.

SOUR CREAM GRAVY

Measure the meat broth remaining in skillet; if necessary, add enough water to measure 1 cup. Mix 1 cup dairy sour cream, 1 tablespoon flour and 1 teaspoon dill weed in the skillet. Gradually stir in the meat broth and heat just to boiling, stirring constantly.

Dilled Pot Roast

SWEDISH MEATBALLS

1 pound ground beef
½ pound ground lean pork
½ cup minced onion
¾ cup dry bread crumbs
1 tablespoon snipped parsley
2 teaspoons salt
⅛ teaspoon pepper
1 teaspoon Worcestershire sauce
1 egg
½ cup milk
¼ cup salad oil
¼ cup all-purpose flour
1 teaspoon paprika
½ teaspoon salt
⅛ teaspoon pepper
2 cups water
¾ cup dairy sour cream

Mix thoroughly beef, pork, onion, bread crumbs, parsley, 2 teaspoons salt, ⅛ teaspoon pepper, the Worcestershire sauce, egg and milk.

Shape the mixture by rounded tablespoonfuls into small balls (about the size of walnuts). Heat salad oil in a large skillet and slowly brown and cook meatballs until they're done. Remove the meatballs from the skillet and keep warm.

Blend flour, paprika, ½ teaspoon salt and ⅛ teaspoon pepper into the oil in the skillet. Cook over low heat, stirring until the mixture is smooth and bubbly.

Stir in water and heat to boiling, stirring constantly. Boil and stir 1 minute.

Reduce heat and gradually stir in sour cream, mixing until smooth. Add meatballs; heat through.

6 TO 8 SERVINGS.

BAKED MEATBALLS

1 pound ground beef
⅓ cup chopped onion
½ cup dry bread crumbs
1 teaspoon salt
⅛ teaspoon pepper
½ teaspoon Worcestershire sauce
1 egg
¼ cup milk

Heat oven to 400°. Mix all the ingredients thoroughly and shape the mixture into 1-inch balls. (Use a small ice-cream scoop if you have one. It's a timesaver—and it makes meatballs of uniform size.)

Place the meatballs in an ungreased jelly roll pan, 15½ × 10½ × 1 inch. Bake 10 minutes or until done.

4 TO 6 SERVINGS.

CHEESE-CRUSTED
MEATBALL CASSEROLE

1 pound ground beef
¼ cup dry bread crumbs
⅔ cup chopped onion
2 teaspoons salt
Dash of pepper
½ cup milk
2 tablespoons butter or margarine
⅓ cup chopped onion
¼ cup chopped green pepper
1 can (16 ounces) tomatoes
1 can (6 ounces) tomato paste
½ cup sliced pimiento-stuffed olives
¼ teaspoon pepper
¼ teaspoon garlic salt
⅛ teaspoon crushed red pepper or a pinch of cayenne red pepper
Cheese Pastry (below)

Mix ground beef, bread crumbs, ⅔ cup onion, the salt, a dash of pepper and the milk. Shape the mixture into 20 meatballs. Melt butter in a large skillet and brown meatballs.

Push the meatballs to the side of the skillet and add ⅓ cup onion and the green pepper. Cook and stir until the vegetables are tender. Stir in tomatoes, tomato paste, olives, ¼ teaspoon pepper, the garlic salt and red pepper. Heat to boiling over medium heat. Reduce heat and keep warm while preparing the pastry.

Heat oven to 425°. Prepare Cheese Pastry. Pour the hot meat mixture into an ungreased baking dish, 8×8×2 inches. Cut slits in pastry; place over hot meat mixture and flute the edge. Bake 30 minutes.

6 SERVINGS.

CHEESE PASTRY

1 cup all-purpose flour*
½ teaspoon salt
½ cup shredded Cheddar cheese
⅓ cup plus 1 tablespoon shortening
2 to 3 tablespoons cold water

Measure flour, salt and cheese into a bowl. Cut in shortening thoroughly with a pastry blender. Sprinkle in the water, 1 tablespoon at a time, mixing until all flour is moistened and dough almost cleans the side of the bowl (1 to 2 teaspoons water can be added if needed).

Gather the dough into a ball; shape into a flattened round on a lightly floured cloth-covered board. Roll into a 10-inch square.

Crust plus! This versatile cheese pastry and a touch of imagination can do wonders. Remember it for your next deep-dish apple pie or for a tasty topper on beef stew.

Or roll out, cut into strips and sprinkle with caraway seed, poppy seed or paprika; bake 8 to 10 minutes in a 450° oven. *Voilà!* Crisp cheese sticks to use as hors d'oeuvres or as crunchy accompaniments for a soup or salad.

*If using self-rising flour, omit salt. Pie crusts made with self-rising flour differ in flavor and texture from those made with plain flour.

FIESTA TAMALE PIE

1 pound ground beef
¼ pound bulk pork sausage
1 small onion, chopped
1 clove garlic, minced
1 can (16 ounces) tomatoes
1 can (16 ounces) whole kernel corn, drained
20 to 24 pitted ripe olives
1½ teaspoons salt
2 to 3 teaspoons chili powder
1 cup cornmeal
1 cup milk
2 eggs, well beaten
1 cup shredded American cheese

Heat oven to 350°. In a large skillet, cook and stir ground beef, pork sausage, onion and garlic until meat is brown and onion is tender. Drain off fat. Stir in the tomatoes, corn, olives and seasonings and heat to boiling.

Pour into an ungreased baking dish, 8×8×2 or 11½×7½×1½ inches, or a 2-quart casserole. Mix cornmeal, milk and eggs and pour over meat mixture. Sprinkle the cheese on top and bake 50 to 60 minutes or until golden brown.

6 TO 8 SERVINGS.

Note: The meat mixture can be prepared ahead of time and kept, covered, in the refrigerator.

A hearty casserole classic, so savory and spicy that it really needs a crisp green or chilled fruit salad as a go-along. Or try a rainbow of sherbet balls as the cool after-taster.

QUICK VEGETABLE SOUP

1 pound ground beef
3 cups water
1 cup cut-up carrots
1 cup diced celery
1 cup cubed pared potatoes
2 medium onions, chopped
  (about 1 cup)
1 can (28 ounces) tomatoes
2 teaspoons salt
1 teaspoon bottled brown bouquet
  sauce
¼ teaspoon pepper
1 bay leaf
⅛ teaspoon basil

Cook and stir ground beef in a large saucepan until brown. Drain off fat. Stir in the remaining ingredients and heat to boiling. Reduce heat. Cover and simmer just until the vegetables are tender, about 20 minutes.

6 SERVINGS.

HAMBURGER STROGANOFF

3 pounds ground beef
3 medium onions, chopped
2 cloves garlic, minced
2 teaspoons salt
½ teaspoon pepper
2 cans (6 ounces each) sliced
  mushrooms, drained
3 cans (10¾ ounces each)
  condensed cream of chicken
  soup
3 cups dairy sour cream or
  unflavored yogurt
12 ounces noodles, cooked and
  drained
  Snipped parsley

Cook and stir ground beef, onion and garlic in a Dutch oven or large roasting pan until meat is brown and onion is tender. Spoon off excess fat. Stir in salt, pepper, mushrooms and soup and heat to boiling, stirring constantly. Reduce heat and simmer uncovered 10 minutes.

Gradually stir in the sour cream and heat through. (Do not allow the mixture to boil or cream may curdle.) Spoon meat mixture over hot noodles and sprinkle with parsley.

12 SERVINGS (⅔ CUP NOODLES AND 1 CUP MEAT MIXTURE PER SERVING).

2 bananas, peeled and quartered
1 can (8 ounces) peach halves
1 can (8 ounces) pear halves
12 maraschino cherries, halved
¼ teaspoon pumpkin pie spice
2- to 3-pound canned* or fully
    cooked boneless smoked ham
4 to 6 medium sweet potatoes,
    cooked, peeled and halved, or
    1 can (23 ounces) vacuum-pack
    sweet potatoes, drained
1 cup brown sugar (packed)
1 teaspoon dry mustard

*Remove gelatin from canned ham before baking.

HAM AND SPICED FRUITS

Combine bananas, peach halves (with syrup), pear halves (with syrup), cherries and pumpkin pie spice. Pour off ½ cup syrup and reserve for the glaze. Refrigerate the fruit.

Heat oven to 350°. Place ham in an ungreased baking dish, 11½ × 7½ × 1½ inches, and arrange sweet potato halves around ham. Mix brown sugar, reserved fruit syrup and dry mustard; pour over the ham and potatoes. Bake uncovered 1 hour, basting ham and potatoes with the syrup several times.

Drain the spiced fruits and arrange attractively on and around the ham. Bake uncovered until fruits are heated through, about 15 minutes.

4 TO 6 SERVINGS.

1 envelope (about 1½ ounces)
    onion soup mix
5- pound pork loin roast
½ cup water
¼ cup all-purpose flour

We guarantee you've never tasted a pork roast as moist and delicious as this one. And it's so easy to make a smooth gravy with the rich drippings—if you remember to add the flour to the water, never the reverse. (With quick-mixing flour, it's even easier—just *stir* it in.)

PORK ROAST WITH ONION GRAVY

Place a 30 × 18-inch piece of heavy-duty aluminum foil in a baking pan, 13 × 9 × 2 inches. Sprinkle soup mix in the center of foil. Trim excess fat from roast. Place roast fat side down on the soup mix. Fold foil over and seal securely, folding up the ends. Cook in 300° oven 3½ hours.

Open the foil wrapping and remove the meat to a platter; keep warm while making the gravy. Skim excess fat from the meat drippings in the foil. Measure the drippings and add enough water to measure 2 cups. Pour into the pan.

Shake water and flour in a covered jar. Stir flour mixture slowly into liquid in the pan. Heat to boiling, stirring constantly. Boil and stir 1 minute.

6 TO 8 SERVINGS.

SWEET 'N SOUR PORK

3¾ pounds pork shoulder
¾ cup all-purpose flour*
1 tablespoon plus 1 teaspoon
    ginger
½ cup salad oil
2 cans (13¼ ounces each)
    pineapple chunks, drained
    (reserve syrup)
½ cup vinegar
½ cup soy sauce
1 tablespoon Worcestershire sauce
¾ cup sugar
1 tablespoon salt
¾ teaspoon pepper
2 small green peppers, cut into
    strips
1 can (16 ounces) bean sprouts,
    drained
1 can (8 ounces) water chestnuts,
    drained and thinly sliced
2 tablespoons chili sauce
    Easy Oven Rice (below)

*If using self-rising flour, decrease salt to 2¼ teaspoons.

Cut the meat into 1-inch cubes, trimming off any excess fat. Mix half the flour with the ginger; coat meat thoroughly with the flour mixture. Heat oil in a large skillet or Dutch oven and brown meat, about a third at a time, over medium heat. Remove meat and set aside.

Add enough water to the reserved pineapple syrup to measure 1¾ cups and gradually stir into the remaining flour. Stir pineapple syrup mixture, vinegar, soy sauce and Worcestershire sauce into the fat in skillet.

Heat to boiling, stirring constantly. Boil and stir 1 minute. Stir in sugar, salt, pepper and meat. Reduce heat. Cover and simmer until the meat is tender, about 1 hour, stirring occasionally.

Add pineapple and green peppers and cook uncovered 10 minutes. Stir in bean sprouts, water chestnuts and chili sauce and heat through, about 5 minutes. Serve over the hot rice.

8 TO 10 SERVINGS.

EASY OVEN RICE
4 cups boiling water
2 cups uncooked regular rice
2 teaspoons salt

Heat oven to 350°. Mix ingredients thoroughly in an ungreased 2-quart casserole or in a baking dish, 13 × 9 × 2 inches. Cover tightly. Bake 25 to 30 minutes or until the liquid is absorbed and the rice is tender.

6 CUPS COOKED RICE.

PORK CUTLETS MORNAY

6 pork sirloin cutlets
2 eggs, beaten
½ cup dry bread crumbs
¼ cup shortening or salad oil
2 tablespoons water
6 tablespoons tomato sauce or
   catsup
   Mornay Sauce (below)
½ cup shredded Cheddar cheese
   Paprika

Dip the cutlets in egg, then coat with bread crumbs. Melt shortening in a large skillet and brown meat over medium heat. Add water and reduce heat. Cover and cook over low heat until done, about 30 minutes.

Arrange meat in an ungreased baking dish, 13½ × 9 × 2 inches. Top each cutlet with 1 tablespoon tomato sauce. Spoon Mornay Sauce on meat and sprinkle with the cheese and paprika.

Set oven control at broil and/or 550°. Broil cutlets 6 to 7 inches from heat until cheese is melted and sauce is bubbly around edges.

6 SERVINGS.

MORNAY SAUCE
1 tablespoon butter or margarine
1 tablespoon flour
⅛ teaspoon each salt, nutmeg
   and cayenne red pepper
½ cup chicken broth*
½ cup light cream
½ cup shredded Cheddar cheese

Melt butter in a small saucepan. Blend in flour and seasonings. Cook over low heat, stirring constantly, until the mixture is smooth and bubbly. Immediately stir in chicken broth and light cream. Heat to boiling, stirring constantly. Boil and stir 1 minute. Stir in cheese until melted.

*Chicken broth can be made by dissolving ½ teaspoon instant chicken bouillon in ½ cup boiling water.

PORK CHOPS SUPREME

2 tablespoons shortening
6 pork loin or rib chops,
  ¾ to 1 inch thick
  Salt and pepper
6 thin onion slices
6 thin lemon slices
6 tablespoons brown sugar
6 tablespoons catsup

Melt shortening in a large skillet and brown chops over medium heat. Season chops with salt and pepper and place them in a shallow baking pan or baking dish. Top each chop with an onion slice, a lemon slice, 1 tablespoon brown sugar and 1 tablespoon catsup.

Cover and cook in a 350° oven 30 minutes. Uncover and cook until done, about 30 minutes longer —basting the chops occasionally.

6 SERVINGS.

VARIATION

Party Pork Chops: Use 1½- to 2-inch chops. Cover and cook 1 hour. Uncover and, basting the chops occasionally, cook until done, 30 minutes longer.

Here's a great favorite with the male guests in our dining room. The menu often features lemon broccoli, hot corn muffins and strawberry shortcake.

EGGPLANT PARMIGIANA

Italian Sauce (below)
1 medium eggplant (1¼ to 1½ pounds)
1 package (6 ounces) sliced mozzarella cheese (reserve 2 slices)
½ cup grated Parmesan cheese

Prepare Italian Sauce. Heat oven to 350°. Pare eggplant and cut into ¼-inch slices. Alternate layers of eggplant slices with mozzarella cheese slices and Italian Sauce in an ungreased 2-quart casserole. Sprinkle with Parmesan cheese and top with the reserved mozzarella.

Cover and bake 50 minutes. Uncover and bake 10 minutes longer or until the cheese is melted and light brown.

6 SERVINGS.

ITALIAN SAUCE
1 pound Italian or bulk pork sausage
1 can (16 ounces) tomatoes
1 can (6 ounces) tomato paste
1 clove garlic, minced
2 tablespoons snipped parsley
1 tablespoon minced onion
½ teaspoon salt
½ teaspoon oregano
¼ teaspoon pepper

Cook and stir sausage in a large skillet until brown. Drain off fat. Stir in the remaining ingredients. Cover and simmer 45 minutes.

3½ CUPS.

4½- to 5-pound stewing chicken, cut up
1 cup all-purpose flour*
2 teaspoons salt
2 teaspoons paprika
¼ teaspoon pepper
Shortening or salad oil
1 cup water
3 tablespoons flour
Milk
Dumplings (below)

*If using self-rising flour, decrease salt to 1 teaspoon.

Remember the old dumpling recipes that warned: "Do not peek while they cook"? Well, we literally uncovered a new method for making dumplings—and you can peek!

If you like, mix a couple of tablespoons of snipped chives or parsley into the dumpling batter. Or add a subtle boost of flavor to the simmering chicken broth instead—with sliced onions, celery tops, carrot slices or your favorite herbs.

CHICKEN FRICASSEE WITH DUMPLINGS

Wash the chicken and pat dry. Mix 1 cup flour, the salt, paprika and pepper; coat chicken with the flour mixture. Heat a thin layer of shortening in a large skillet or Dutch oven and brown chicken over medium heat. Drain off fat and reserve.

Add water to the skillet. Cover and simmer until the chicken is fork-tender, 2½ to 3½ hours, adding more water if necessary. Remove the chicken and keep warm while making the gravy. Pour the liquid from skillet and reserve.

To make the gravy, heat 3 tablespoons of the reserved fat in skillet. Blend in 3 tablespoons flour. Cook over low heat, stirring until the mixture is smooth and bubbly. Remove from heat. Add enough milk to the reserved liquid to measure 3 cups and pour into the skillet. Heat to boiling, stirring constantly. Boil and stir 1 minute.

Return chicken to the gravy in the skillet. Prepare dough for Dumplings and drop by spoonfuls onto hot chicken. Cook uncovered 10 minutes. Cover and cook 20 minutes longer.

6 TO 8 SERVINGS.

DUMPLINGS

1½ cups all-purpose flour**
2 teaspoons baking powder
¾ teaspoon salt
3 tablespoons shortening
¾ cup milk

Measure flour, baking powder and salt into a bowl. Cut in shortening thoroughly with a pastry blender until mixture looks like meal. Stir in the milk.

**If using self-rising flour, omit baking powder and salt.

Oven-fried Chicken

OVEN-FRIED CHICKEN

2½ to 3 pounds broiler-fryer
   chicken pieces
¼ cup shortening
¼ cup butter or margarine
½ cup all-purpose flour*
1 teaspoon salt
1 teaspoon paprika
¼ teaspoon pepper

*If using self-rising flour, decrease salt to ½ teaspoon.

Heat oven to 425°. Wash the chicken and pat dry. Melt shortening and butter in a baking pan, 13 × 9 × 2 inches, in the oven.

Mix flour, salt, paprika and pepper; coat chicken thoroughly with the flour mixture. Place chicken skin side down in the pan. Bake uncovered 30 minutes. Turn the chicken and bake until thickest pieces are fork-tender, 20 to 30 minutes longer.

4 SERVINGS.

VARIATION

Crunchy Oven-fried Chicken: Substitute 3 cups corn puffs cereal, crushed, for the flour mixture. Roll chicken in the melted shortening and butter, then coat with the cereal.

ALMOND OVEN-FRIED CHICKEN

2 broiler-fryer chickens (2½
   pounds each), cut up
   Salt
2 tablespoons butter or margarine
2 tablespoons shortening
1 cup all-purpose flour*
2 teaspoons salt
2 teaspoons paprika
¼ teaspoon pepper
2 eggs, slightly beaten
3 tablespoons milk
2 cups finely chopped blanched
   almonds
¼ cup butter or margarine, melted

*If using self-rising flour, decrease the 2 teaspoons salt to 1 teaspoon.

Heat oven to 400°. Wash the chicken and pat dry. Remove skin from all pieces except the wings. Sprinkle chicken lightly with salt.

Melt 2 tablespoons butter and the shortening in a jelly roll pan, 15½ × 10½ × 1 inch, in the oven. Mix flour, 2 teaspoons salt, the paprika and pepper. Combine eggs and milk. Coat chicken with the flour mixture; dip into egg and milk and roll in nuts. Place chicken bone side down in the pan and drizzle with melted butter. Bake uncovered until thickest pieces are fork-tender, about 1 hour.

6 SERVINGS.

SHERRIED CHICKEN SUPREME

2 tablespoons butter or margarine
2 tablespoons salad oil
6 large chicken breast halves
   (2½ to 3 pounds)
1 can (10¾ ounces) condensed
   cream of chicken soup
½ cup light cream
½ cup dry sherry or, if desired,
   ½ cup apple juice plus 3
   tablespoons sherry flavoring
1 can (13¼ ounces) pineapple
   chunks, drained
½ cup sliced seedless green grapes
1 can (6 ounces) sliced mushrooms,
   drained

Heat oven to 350°. Heat butter and oil in a baking dish, 13½×9×2 inches. Place chicken pieces skin side up in the baking dish and bake uncovered 1 hour.

Heat soup, light cream and sherry in a saucepan, stirring occasionally. Stir in pineapple, grapes and mushrooms.

Remove the baking dish from the oven and drain off fat. Pour the soup mixture over chicken. Cover with aluminum foil and continue baking until chicken is fork-tender, 15 to 20 minutes longer. Garnish with clusters of seedless green grapes.

6 SERVINGS.

CHICKEN-WILD RICE CASSEROLE

½ cup butter or margarine
½ cup all-purpose flour*
2½ teaspoons salt
¼ teaspoon pepper
1½ cups chicken broth**
2¼ cups milk
2¼ cups cooked wild or white
   rice
3 cups cut-up cooked chicken
2 jars (4½ ounces each) sliced
   mushrooms, drained
½ cup chopped green pepper
1 jar (2 ounces) sliced pimiento,
   drained
⅓ cup slivered almonds
   Snipped parsley

*If using self-rising flour, decrease salt to 2 teaspoons.

**Chicken broth can be made by dissolving 1½ teaspoons instant chicken bouillon in 1½ cups boiling water, or use canned chicken broth.

Heat oven to 350°. Melt butter in a large skillet or Dutch oven. Blend in flour, salt and pepper. Cook over low heat, stirring until mixture is smooth and bubbly. Immediately stir in chicken broth and milk. Heat to boiling, stirring constantly. Boil and stir 1 minute.

Stir in rice, chicken, mushrooms, green pepper, pimiento and almonds. Pour into a greased baking dish, 13½×9×2 inches. Bake 40 to 45 minutes. Sprinkle with parsley.

12 SERVINGS (3-INCH SQUARE PER PORTION).

VARIATION

Turkey-Wild Rice Casserole: Substitute 3 cups cut-up cooked turkey for the chicken.

CHICKEN-SAUSAGE PIES

½ **pound bulk pork sausage**
   Savory Pastry (below)
1 **jar (2½ ounces) sliced**
   mushrooms, drained (reserve
   liquid)
¼ **cup butter or margarine**
⅓ **cup all-purpose flour**
¼ **teaspoon salt**
1 **can (13¾ ounces) chicken**
   broth (1⅔ cups)
1 **cup light cream**
2 **cups cut-up cooked chicken**

Pretty up the pastry by making cross-slits or cutouts in the center. Or try one of our dining room favorites: old-fashioned Chicken Littles. Roll any leftover pastry about ¼ inch thick and cut with a small chicken-shaped cookie cutter (or trace around a pattern with a knife). Insert a wooden pick halfway into the base of each "chicken" and prick with a fork. Bake right along with the rounds, only keep these in the oven a bit longer—10 to 15 minutes in all, or until golden brown. Then simply stand a Chicken Little upright in the center of each crust.

For a touch of color, garnish the pies with parsley and pimiento strips.

Heat oven to 400°. Shape pork sausage into ½-inch balls. Place on rack in broiler pan and bake 15 minutes. Remove from the oven and set aside.

Increase the oven temperature to 425°. Prepare Savory Pastry and place the pastry rounds on an ungreased baking sheet; prick thoroughly with a fork. Bake 8 to 10 minutes or until golden brown.

Cook and stir mushrooms in butter 5 minutes. Stir in flour and salt and cook over low heat, stirring until mixture is bubbly. Immediately stir in broth, cream and the reserved liquid. Heat to boiling, stirring constantly. Boil and stir 1 minute.

Divide sausage balls and chicken among the 6 ungreased casseroles. Pour the cream sauce over meat. Top each casserole with a baked pastry round. Heat in 425° oven until the sauce bubbles.

6 SERVINGS.

SAVORY PASTRY
1 **cup all-purpose flour***
1 **teaspoon celery seed**
½ **teaspoon salt**
½ **teaspoon paprika**
⅓ **cup plus 1 tablespoon shortening**
2 **to 3 tablespoons cold water**

Measure flour, celery seed, salt and paprika into a bowl. Cut in shortening thoroughly. Sprinkle in the water, 1 tablespoon at a time, mixing until dough almost cleans side of bowl.

Gather the dough into a ball and shape into a flattened round. Roll about ⅛ inch thick on a lightly floured cloth-covered board. Cut into 6 rounds to fit the tops of 1½-cup individual casseroles.

*If using self-rising flour, omit salt.

HOT CHICKEN SUPPER SALAD

2 cups cut-up cooked chicken
2 cups thinly sliced celery
1 cup toasted bread cubes
1 cup mayonnaise
½ cup toasted slivered almonds
2 tablespoons lemon juice
¼ cup chopped onion
½ teaspoon salt
½ cup shredded Cheddar cheese
1 cup toasted bread cubes or
   crushed potato chips

Heat oven to 350°. Combine all ingredients except the cheese and 1 cup bread cubes. Pile into 4 or 5 ungreased individual casseroles or an ungreased 2-quart casserole. Sprinkle with cheese and bread cubes. Bake individual casseroles 20 to 25 minutes, 2-quart casserole 30 to 35 minutes or until hot and bubbly.

4 OR 5 SERVINGS.

VARIATION

Hot Tuna Supper Salad: Substitute 2 cans (6½ ounces each) tuna, drained, for the chicken.

CHICKEN CLUB SALAD

Barbecue Salad Dressing (below)
1 head lettuce, washed and chilled
8 to 10 slices bacon, crisply fried
2 cups cubed cooked chicken,
   chilled
2 large tomatoes, cut into eighths
1 hard-cooked egg, sliced

Prepare Barbecue Salad Dressing. Tear the lettuce into bite-size pieces (about 6 cups). Break bacon into large pieces.

Just before serving, add bacon and chicken to the lettuce and toss lightly. Garnish with tomato wedges and egg slices. Serve with the salad dressing.

4 SERVINGS.

BARBECUE SALAD DRESSING

½ cup mayonnaise or salad dressing
¼ cup barbecue sauce
1 tablespoon instant minced onion
1 tablespoon lemon juice
½ teaspoon salt
¼ teaspoon pepper

Blend all ingredients. Cover and refrigerate.

ABOUT ¾ CUP.

CHICKEN SALAD
IN PINEAPPLE BOATS

2 fresh pineapples
2½ cups cut-up cooked chicken
    or turkey
¾ cup diced celery
¾ cup mayonnaise or salad
    dressing
2 tablespoons chopped chutney
1 teaspoon curry powder
1 medium banana
⅓ cup salted peanuts
½ cup flaked coconut
1 can (11 ounces) mandarin
    orange segments, drained

Quarter each pineapple, cutting right through the green top. Remove fruit; core and cut into chunks. Drain the pineapple shells on paper towels.

Combine pineapple chunks, chicken and celery in a large bowl. For the dressing, mix mayonnaise, chutney and curry powder in another bowl. Cover both bowls and chill at least 1 hour.

Just before serving, drain the liquid from the chicken mixture. Slice banana into the bowl, then add peanuts and the dressing. Toss until all ingredients are well coated.

Spoon the salad into the pineapple shells and sprinkle each with coconut. Garnish with orange segments.

8 SERVINGS.

Chicken salad with a tropical touch. For "clear sailing," use a grapefruit knife to cut along the edge of the pineapple boat.

CREOLE FLOUNDER

2 pounds fresh or frozen flounder
  fillets
1½ cups chopped tomatoes
½ cup chopped green pepper
⅓ cup lemon juice
1 tablespoon salad oil
2 teaspoons salt
2 teaspoons minced onion
1 teaspoon basil leaves
¼ teaspoon coarsely ground black
  pepper
4 drops red pepper sauce

Thaw the fillets if they're frozen. Heat oven to 500°. Place fillets in a single layer in an ungreased baking dish, 13½×9×2 inches. Mix the remaining ingredients and spoon over fillets. Bake until fish flakes easily with a fork, 5 to 8 minutes. Remove fillets to a warm platter. Garnish with tomato wedges and green pepper rings.

6 SERVINGS.

CRABMEAT AVOCADO

4 ripe avocados
  Lemon juice
  Salt
1 can (3 ounces) chopped
  mushrooms, drained
2 tablespoons butter or margarine
2 tablespoons flour
1 teaspoon salt
¼ teaspoon white pepper
1 cup light cream
1 egg yolk, beaten
¼ cup chopped ripe olives
2 cans (7½ ounces each)
  crabmeat, drained and cartilage
  removed
  Grated Parmesan cheese

Heat oven to 325°. Cut each unpeeled avocado in half. Brush with lemon juice (to prevent discoloration) and sprinkle with salt. Place in ½ inch of hot water in a baking dish, 13½×9×2 inches.

Cook and stir mushrooms in butter 5 minutes. Stir in flour, 1 teaspoon salt and the pepper. Cook over low heat, stirring until mixture is bubbly. Remove from heat and stir in cream. Heat to boiling, stirring constantly. Remove from heat. Gradually stir part of the hot mixture into egg yolk, then blend into the hot mixture in the saucepan. Stir in olives and crabmeat.

Spoon the crabmeat mixture into the avocado halves and sprinkle with cheese. Bake 20 minutes or until heated through.

8 SERVINGS.

VARIATION

Tuna Avocado: Substitute 2 cans (7 ounces each) tuna, drained, for the crabmeat.

SALMON ROMANOFF

8 ounces uncooked medium
  noodles
1½ cups creamed cottage cheese
1 to 1½ cups dairy sour cream
½ cup finely chopped onion
1 clove garlic, minced
1 to 2 teaspoons Worcestershire
  sauce
  Dash of cayenne red pepper
½ teaspoon salt
1 can (16 ounces) salmon,
  drained
½ cup shredded sharp cheese

Heat oven to 325°. Cook the noodles as directed on package; drain. Mix noodles and the remaining ingredients except the sharp cheese.

Pour into a greased 2-quart casserole. Sprinkle with cheese. Bake uncovered 40 minutes. Garnish with parsley and lemon wedges.

6 TO 8 SERVINGS.

AVERY ISLAND DEVILED SHRIMP

Deviled Shrimp Sauce (below)
1 egg, slightly beaten
¼ teaspoon salt
2 cups cleaned cooked shrimp*
½ cup dry bread crumbs
¼ cup butter or margarine
2 cups hot cooked rice

*From 1½ pounds fresh or frozen raw shrimp (in shells), 2 packages (7 ounces each) frozen peeled shrimp or 2 cans (4½ or 5 ounces each) shrimp.

Prepare Deviled Shrimp Sauce. Mix egg and salt. Dip shrimp in egg, then coat with bread crumbs. Melt butter in a skillet and brown shrimp over medium heat. Serve shrimp on rice and pour hot sauce over shrimp.

4 SERVINGS.

DEVILED SHRIMP SAUCE

1 medium onion, chopped
1 clove garlic, minced
2 tablespoons butter or margarine
1 can (10¾ ounces) condensed
  chicken broth
½ cup water
2 tablespoons steak sauce
1½ teaspoons dry mustard
½ teaspoon salt
¼ to ½ teaspoon red pepper sauce
1 to 2 tablespoons lemon juice

Cook and stir onion and garlic in butter until onion is tender. Stir in remaining ingredients except lemon juice. Heat to boiling, stirring occasionally, then simmer 15 minutes. Stir in lemon juice.

TUNA SALAD
IN CARAWAY PUFF BOWL

½ cup water
¼ cup butter or margarine
½ cup all-purpose flour*
⅛ teaspoon salt
½ to 1 teaspoon caraway seed
2 eggs
   Tuna Salad (below)

*If using self-rising flour, omit salt.

This giant cream puff shell makes a spectacular showcase dessert (without the caraway seed, of course). Fill it with a mixture of sweetened whipped cream and strawberries or with scoops of ice cream, sundaed with a sauce. Very impressive!

The salads, too, can solo superbly. All they need is a bed of crisp greens.

Heat oven to 400°. Grease a 9-inch glass pie pan. Heat water and butter to a rolling boil in a medium saucepan. Quickly stir in flour, salt and caraway seed. Stir vigorously over low heat until the mixture forms a ball, about 1 minute. Remove from heat.

Beat in eggs, all at one time, and continue beating until smooth. Spread the batter evenly in the pie pan. (Have batter touching the side of the pan, but do not spread it up the side.) Bake 45 to 50 minutes or until puffed and golden brown.

Just before serving, mound the Tuna Salad in the puff bowl. Garnish with parsley, sliced tomatoes or hard-cooked eggs. To serve, cut into wedges.

6 TO 8 SERVINGS.

TUNA SALAD

2 cans (7 ounces each) tuna, drained
1 cup cut-up celery
½ cup cubed avocado or ½ cup
   chopped green or ripe olives
¼ cup chopped onion
1 tablespoon lemon juice
3 hard-cooked eggs, cut up
½ teaspoon curry powder, if desired
¾ to 1 cup mayonnaise

Combine all ingredients except the mayonnaise. Cover and chill. Just before serving, fold mayonnaise into the tuna mixture.

VARIATIONS

Chicken Salad: Substitute 2 cups cut-up cooked chicken for the tuna.

Shrimp Salad: Substitute 2 cans (4½ ounces each) shrimp, rinsed and drained, for the tuna.

CHEESE STRATA

⅓ cup soft butter or margarine
1 clove garlic, crushed
½ teaspoon dry mustard
10 slices white bread, crusts removed
2 cups shredded sharp Cheddar cheese
2 tablespoons chopped onion
2 tablespoons snipped parsley
1 teaspoon salt
½ teaspoon Worcestershire sauce
⅛ teaspoon pepper
Dash of cayenne red pepper
4 eggs
2⅓ cups milk
⅔ cup dry white wine*

*If you prefer, omit the wine and increase milk to 2½ cups.

Mix butter, garlic and mustard and spread on one side of each bread slice. Cut each slice into thirds. Line the bottom and sides of an ungreased baking dish, 8×8×2 inches, with some of the bread slices, buttered sides down.

Mix cheese, onion, parsley, salt, Worcestershire sauce, pepper and cayenne red pepper; spread evenly in the baking dish. Top with the remaining bread slices, buttered sides up. Beat eggs and blend in the milk and wine; pour over the bread. Cover and refrigerate at least 2 hours.

Heat oven to 325°. Bake uncovered until golden brown, about 1¼ hours. (To test, a knife inserted in center will come out clean.) Let stand 10 minutes before serving.

9 SERVINGS.

QUICHE LORRAINE

Pastry for 9-inch One-crust Pie (page 123)
12 slices bacon (½ pound), crisply fried and crumbled
1 cup shredded natural Swiss cheese (about 4 ounces)
⅓ cup minced onion
4 eggs
2 cups whipping cream or light cream
¾ teaspoon salt
¼ teaspoon sugar
⅛ teaspoon cayenne red pepper

Heat oven to 425°. Prepare the pastry. Sprinkle bacon, cheese and onion in the pastry-lined pie pan. Beat eggs slightly and blend in the remaining ingredients. Pour the cream mixture into the pie pan.

Bake 15 minutes, then reduce the oven temperature to 300° and bake 30 minutes longer or until a knife inserted 1 inch from the edge comes out clean. Let the pie stand 10 minutes before cutting. Serve in wedges.

6 MAIN-DISH OR 8 APPETIZER SERVINGS.

Salads and Vegetables

Salads and Vegetables

Wherever you take your taste traveling these days, there's no place like back home USA for beauty and bounty in the salad and vegetable department. Only a generation or so ago, fresh produce was a seasonal and sometime thing at our tables. Today, you can pick most fruits and vegetables at the supermarket any day of the year.

You tell us you like your salads lush and versatile. With lettuce, of course, but in variety. With head, Boston, bibb and leaf. But what will you have for color and texture? Think about cucumbers, carrots or avocados, and apples, oranges or grapefruit. Try something different like Hot Spinach Salad or turn to a classic like Kidney Bean. You take your fresh vegetables seriously, too. Especially when it comes to time-honored standbys like Tomatoes Vinaigrette, Chive-buttered Carrots and Zucchini Provençale.

But let's give a grateful nod to canned and frozen fare. We used to make Golden Corn Pudding by shaving the kernels off ears of fresh-picked corn. How much simpler it is today to use canned corn—and get the same good results. And what would we ever do without the canned fruits for 24-Hour Salad? It's an elegant choice to serve the whole year round. Cranberry Relish Salad has been streamlined, too. If you like, you can save an hour or so by starting off with a frozen relish instead of fresh berries.

On the following pages you'll find a typically American blend of old-time standards and new-found favorites. It's an intriguing collection of recipes—capable of coddling the most hesitant vegetable eater while still intriguing the adventurous aficionado.

On the preceding pages:
French Fried Onion Rings,
Old-fashioned Potato Salad,
Tomatoes Vinaigrette,
Chive-buttered Carrots

FRENCH DRESSING

1 cup olive oil or salad oil
¼ cup vinegar
¼ cup lemon juice
1 teaspoon salt
½ teaspoon dry mustard
½ teaspoon paprika

Shake all ingredients in a tightly covered jar; refrigerate. Shake again just before serving.

1½ CUPS.

SWEET GARLIC DRESSING

¼ cup sugar
½ teaspoon salt
1 clove garlic, crushed
  Dash of pepper
2 to 3 tablespoons olive oil
  or salad oil
¼ cup vinegar

Shake all ingredients in a tightly covered jar. Refrigerate several hours to blend flavors. Shake again just before serving. This sweet oil and vinegar dressing is especially good with sliced tomatoes, a slaw or a tossed green salad.

ABOUT ½ CUP.

BLUE CHEESE DRESSING

1 cup dairy sour cream
2 green onions, finely chopped
2 tablespoons mayonnaise
2 tablespoons lemon juice
½ cup crumbled blue cheese
  Salt and pepper to taste

Mix all ingredients in a small bowl. Cover and refrigerate at least 2 hours to blend flavors. A perfect accent for any salad of greens or vegetables.

ABOUT 1½ CUPS.

COOKED SALAD DRESSING

¼ cup all-purpose flour
2 tablespoons sugar
1 teaspoon salt
1 teaspoon dry mustard
2 egg yolks
1½ cups milk
⅓ cup vinegar
1 tablespoon butter or margarine

Mix flour, sugar, salt and mustard in a medium saucepan. Beat egg yolks slightly and stir in milk. Stir the egg-milk mixture into the flour mixture.

Cook over medium heat, stirring constantly, until the mixture thickens and boils. Boil and stir 1 minute. Remove from heat and stir in vinegar and butter. Cool thoroughly. Try mixing with an equal amount of dairy sour cream or whipped cream.

ABOUT 2 CUPS.

GOURMET TOSSED GREEN SALAD

1 large head lettuce, washed and chilled
¼ pound fresh mushrooms, sliced (about 2 cups)
1 small cauliflower, separated into tiny flowerets (about 2½ cups)
1 small Bermuda onion, sliced thinly and separated into rings
1 medium green pepper, diced (about ⅔ cup)
½ cup sliced pimiento-stuffed green olives
½ cup crumbled blue cheese
 Classic French Dressing (right)

Tear the lettuce into bite-size pieces (about 10 cups). Add remaining ingredients except Classic French Dressing and toss. Cover and chill thoroughly, at least 1 hour. Just before serving, toss with the dressing.

8 TO 10 SERVINGS.

CLASSIC FRENCH DRESSING

¼ cup olive oil, salad oil or combination
2 tablespoons wine or tarragon vinegar
1 small clove garlic, crushed
¾ teaspoon salt
¼ teaspoon monosodium glutamate
 Generous dash of freshly ground pepper

Just before serving, toss the salad with oil until the greens glisten. Mix vinegar and seasonings thoroughly. Pour over the salad and toss.

TOSSED ARTICHOKE AND OLIVE SALAD

8 ounces spinach
1 large head lettuce, washed and chilled
2 jars (6 ounces each) marinated artichoke hearts
2 cans (3⅞ ounces each) pitted ripe olives, drained
 French Dressing (page 39) or bottled herb salad dressing

Wash spinach; remove the stems and dry the leaves. Tear the spinach leaves and lettuce into bite-size pieces (about 12 cups). For an easy tossing trick, divide the greens evenly between 2 large plastic bags and refrigerate.

Just before serving, add 1 jar artichoke hearts (with the liquid), 1 can olives and ⅓ cup salad dressing to each bag. Close the bags tightly and shake until the greens are well coated with dressing.

12 SERVINGS.

HOT SPINACH SALAD

10 to 12 ounces fresh spinach
1 clove garlic, peeled and slivered
⅓ cup salad oil
¼ cup red wine vinegar
¼ teaspoon salt
　Dash of pepper
2 hard-cooked eggs, chopped
3 slices bacon, crisply fried and
　crumbled

Wash spinach; remove the stems and dry the leaves. Tear into bite-size pieces (about 10 cups) and refrigerate. Let garlic stand in oil 1 hour, then remove garlic.

Just before serving, heat oil, vinegar, salt and pepper in a chafing dish or small saucepan, stirring occasionally. Toss the hot dressing with the spinach until leaves are well coated. Sprinkle chopped eggs and bacon over the salad and toss lightly.

4 TO 6 SERVINGS.

GRANDMOTHER'S LETTUCE SALAD

2 bunches leaf lettuce, washed
　and chilled
½ cup light cream (20%)
1 to 1½ tablespoons sugar
¼ teaspoon salt
3 to 4 tablespoons vinegar

Tear the leaf lettuce into bite-size pieces (about 6 cups). Just before serving, mix light cream, sugar, salt and vinegar. Pour over the lettuce and toss.

5 OR 6 SERVINGS.

CARROT-RAISIN SALAD

2 cups finely shredded carrots
　(3 to 4 medium)
⅓ cup raisins
1 tablespoon snipped chives
¼ teaspoon salt
　Cooked Salad Dressing (page 39)
　or mayonnaise

Combine carrots, raisins, chives and salt in a bowl. Add just enough salad dressing to moisten the ingredients and toss lightly. We like to serve this salad in lettuce cups and garnished with parsley.

4 OR 5 SERVINGS.

Note: Use your blender to chop the carrots. Cut them into ½-inch slices. Place half the carrot slices in blender and add water just to cover carrots.

Cover and follow manufacturer's instructions or run just long enough to finely chop carrots (3 to 5 seconds). Empty carrots into a strainer and drain thoroughly. Repeat with the remaining carrots.

CABBAGE-RED APPLE SALAD

5 cups shredded or finely
 chopped cabbage (about
 1 small head)
1 unpared red apple, diced
½ cup sliced celery
1 teaspoon salt
 Mayonnaise or Cooked Salad
 Dressing (page 39)

Combine cabbage, apple, celery and salt in a bowl. Add just enough mayonnaise to moisten and toss. Chill before serving.

6 TO 8 SERVINGS.

VARIATION

Cabbage-Pineapple Salad: Add 1 can (8¼ ounces) crushed pineapple, drained, and ½ cup miniature marshmallows.

OLD-FASHIONED CABBAGE SLAW

1 teaspoon salt
¼ teaspoon pepper
½ teaspoon dry mustard
½ teaspoon celery seed
2 tablespoons sugar
¼ cup chopped green pepper
1 tablespoon chopped pimiento
1 teaspoon instant minced onion
3 tablespoons salad oil
⅓ cup white vinegar
4 cups finely shredded or chopped
 cabbage (about ½ medium head)

Combine all the ingredients in a large bowl. Cover and chill thoroughly, at least 3 hours.

Just before serving, drain the cabbage. Garnish with watercress and sliced pimiento-stuffed olives.

6 SERVINGS.

KIDNEY BEAN SALAD

1 can (20 ounces) kidney beans,
 drained
¼ cup diced celery
3 dill or sweet pickles, chopped
1 small onion, minced
½ teaspoon salt
⅛ teaspoon pepper
 About ¼ cup mayonnaise or
 dairy sour cream
2 hard-cooked eggs, sliced

Mix all ingredients except the eggs. Add eggs and toss lightly. Chill thoroughly, at least 4 hours. Serve the salad on a bed of crisp greens and garnish with grated cheese or onion rings.

6 SERVINGS.

TOMATOES VINAIGRETTE

8 to 12 thick slices tomato or
  peeled small tomatoes
1 cup olive oil or salad oil
⅓ cup wine vinegar
2 teaspoons oregano leaves
1 teaspoon salt
½ teaspoon pepper
½ teaspoon dry mustard
2 cloves garlic, crushed
  Crisp lettuce leaves
  Minced green onion
  Snipped parsley

If using small tomatoes, cut off the stem ends. Arrange tomatoes in a baking dish, 8×8×2 inches. Shake oil, vinegar, oregano, salt, pepper, mustard and garlic in a tightly covered jar. Pour over the tomatoes. Cover and chill at least 2 hours, spooning the dressing over the tomatoes from time to time.

Just before serving, arrange tomatoes on lettuce leaves. Sprinkle tomatoes with onion and parsley and drizzle some of the dressing on top.

6 TO 8 SERVINGS.

CRANBERRY RELISH SALAD

4 cups cranberries
1½ cups sugar
1 cup chilled whipping cream
2 cups Tokay grapes, halved
  and seeded
1 can (13¼ ounces) crushed
  pineapple, drained
½ cup coarsely chopped walnuts
  or pecans

Finely chop cranberries in a food chopper. Sprinkle sugar over cranberries and let stand 1 hour.

Drain cranberries thoroughly. In a chilled bowl, beat whipping cream until stiff. Combine grapes, pineapple, nuts and cranberries; fold in the whipped cream. Serve the salad in lettuce cups.

This triple-treat recipe can serve as a side-salad, as an accompaniment for poultry and as a dessert.

6 TO 8 SERVINGS.

Note: 1 package (10 ounces) frozen cranberry relish, thawed and drained, can be substituted for the cranberries and sugar.

24-Hour Salad

CUCUMBER RELISH MOLD

1 package (3 ounces) lime-flavored
  gelatin
1 cup drained shredded pared
  cucumber
1 cup thinly sliced celery
3 tablespoons thinly sliced
  green onions
½ teaspoon salt
  Mayonnaise

Prepare gelatin as directed on package except—decrease the water to 1½ cups. Chill until slightly thickened but not set. Fold in the vegetables and salt. Pour into a 4-cup mold or 4 to 6 individual molds. Chill until firm. Unmold onto a lettuce-lined plate and serve with mayonnaise.

4 TO 6 SERVINGS.

24-HOUR SALAD

Old-fashioned Fruit Dressing
(below)
1 can (17 ounces) pitted light
  or dark sweet cherries, drained
2 cans (13¼ ounces each)
  pineapple chunks, drained and
  cut in half (reserve 2
  tablespoons syrup for the
  dressing)
3 oranges, pared, sectioned and
  cut up, or 2 cans (11 ounces
  each) mandarin orange
  segments, drained
1 cup miniature marshmallows

Prepare Old-fashioned Fruit Dressing. Combine fruits and marshmallows. Pour the dressing over the ingredients and toss. Cover and chill 12 to 24 hours.

Serve in a salad bowl or in lettuce cups. If you like, garnish with orange sections and maraschino cherries.

8 TO 10 SERVINGS.

OLD-FASHIONED FRUIT DRESSING

2 eggs, beaten
2 tablespoons sugar
2 tablespoons vinegar or lemon
  juice
2 tablespoons pineapple syrup
  (from the canned pineapple
  chunks)
1 tablespoon butter or margarine
  Dash of salt
¾ cup chilled whipping cream

Combine all ingredients except the whipping cream in a small saucepan. Heat just to boiling, stirring constantly. Remove from heat and cool. In a chilled bowl, beat the cream until stiff. Fold in the egg mixture.

OLD-FASHIONED POTATO SALAD

2 pounds potatoes
(about 6 medium)
¼ cup French Dressing (page 39)
or bottled French or Italian
dressing
1 cup sliced celery
1 cup cubed cucumber
¾ cup minced onion
½ cup thinly sliced radishes
½ cup Cooked Salad Dressing
(page 39) or mayonnaise
½ cup dairy sour cream
1 tablespoon prepared mustard
2 teaspoons lemon juice
1½ teaspoons salt
¼ teaspoon pepper
4 hard-cooked eggs, chopped

Cook the unpared potatoes until tender, 30 to 35 minutes. Drain and cool slightly. Peel the potatoes and cut into cubes.

Pour French Dressing over warm potatoes in a large bowl and toss. Cover and refrigerate at least 4 hours.

Add celery, cucumber, onion and radishes to the potatoes. Mix Cooked Salad Dressing, sour cream, mustard, lemon juice, salt and pepper; pour over the salad and toss. Carefully stir in chopped eggs. Chill. Serve the salad in a bowl lined with crisp lettuce leaves; for color, garnish with parsley, sliced tomatoes or hard-cooked eggs.

6 SERVINGS.

HOT GERMAN POTATO SALAD

3 pounds potatoes
(about 9 medium)
6 slices bacon
¾ cup chopped onion
2 tablespoons flour
2 tablespoons sugar
2 teaspoons salt
½ teaspoon celery seed
Dash of pepper
¾ cup water
⅓ cup vinegar

Pare the potatoes and cook until tender, 30 to 35 minutes. Drain and set aside.

In a large skillet, fry bacon until crisp; remove and drain. Cook and stir chopped onion in bacon drippings until tender and golden. Stir in flour, sugar, salt, celery seed and pepper. Cook over low heat, stirring until bubbly. Remove from heat and stir in water and vinegar. Heat to boiling, stirring constantly. Boil and stir 1 minute. Remove the skillet from heat.

Crumble the bacon and slice the potatoes. Carefully stir bacon and potatoes into the hot mixture in the skillet. Heat through, stirring lightly to coat potato slices.

5 OR 6 SERVINGS.

SKILLET-CREAMED POTATOES

6 pared medium potatoes,
  cooked and drained, or 2 cans
  (16 ounces each) whole potatoes
2 cups dairy sour cream
¼ cup finely chopped onion
2 tablespoons finely chopped
  pimiento-stuffed olives
1 teaspoon salt
½ teaspoon pepper
  Paprika
  Snipped parsley
  Pimiento-stuffed olives, sliced

Cut potatoes into ½-inch cubes. Combine sour cream, onion, chopped olives, salt and pepper in a large skillet. Add potatoes; heat over medium heat, stirring frequently, until the cream bubbles and potatoes are heated through. Garnish with the paprika, parsley and sliced olives.

6 SERVINGS.

TWICE-BAKED POTATOES

4 large baking potatoes
  Shortening
⅓ to ½ cup milk
¼ cup soft butter or margarine
½ teaspoon salt
  Dash of pepper
4 tablespoons finely shredded
  cheese

Heat oven to 375°. Scrub the potatoes; rub them with shortening and prick with a fork. Bake until potatoes are tender, 1 to 1¼ hours.

Increase oven temperature to 400°. Cut a thin slice from the top of each potato and scoop out the inside, leaving a thin shell. Mash potatoes until no lumps remain. Add milk in small amounts, beating after each addition. (The amount of milk needed to make potatoes smooth and fluffy depends on the kind of potatoes used.) Add butter, salt and pepper. Beat until potatoes are light and fluffy.

Fill potato shells with mashed potatoes and sprinkle each with 1 tablespoon shredded cheese. Bake 20 minutes or until golden.

4 SERVINGS.

VARIATION

Pepper or Pimiento Potatoes: Stir ¼ cup finely chopped green pepper or ¼ cup drained chopped pimiento into the mashed potato mixture.

BUFFET POTATOES

2 pounds potatoes
(about 6 medium)
  Pepper
1 teaspoon salt
3 tablespoons snipped parsley
¼ cup chopped onion
¾ cup shredded sharp process
  cheese
3 tablespoons butter or margarine
¾ cup light cream (20%)

Heat oven to 350°. Pare the potatoes and cut into lengthwise strips, ¼ to ⅜ inch wide.

Arrange potatoes in a greased 2-quart casserole in 3 layers, topping each layer with a dash of pepper and ⅓ each of the salt, parsley, onion and cheese. Dot with butter and pour light cream over potatoes. Cover and bake 1 hour. Uncover and bake 30 minutes longer or until the potatoes are tender.

6 TO 8 SERVINGS.

SWEET POTATO-APPLESAUCE BAKE

1 pound sweet potatoes or yams
(about 3 medium) or 1 can
(17 ounces) vacuum-pack sweet
potatoes
½ teaspoon salt
1 can (8 ounces) applesauce
⅓ cup brown sugar (packed)
¼ cup chopped nuts
½ teaspoon cinnamon
2 tablespoons butter or margarine

If using fresh sweet potatoes or yams, cook unpared potatoes until tender, 30 to 35 minutes. Drain and cool slightly. Slip off skins.

Heat oven to 375°. Cut each sweet potato lengthwise in half. Place halves in an ungreased baking dish, 8×8×2 inches. Sprinkle with salt and spread applesauce on potatoes. Mix sugar, nuts and cinnamon and sprinkle over the applesauce. Dot with butter and cover with aluminum foil. Bake 30 minutes or until hot and bubbly.

4 TO 6 SERVINGS.

GOURMET GOLDEN SQUASH

3 pounds Hubbard squash, pared
  and cubed (about 6 cups)
2 tablespoons butter or margarine
1 cup dairy sour cream
½ cup finely chopped onion
1 teaspoon salt
¼ teaspoon pepper

Cook squash until tender, 15 to 20 minutes; drain. Heat oven to 400°. Mash squash and stir in the remaining ingredients. Mound the mixture in an ungreased 1-quart casserole. Bake uncovered 20 minutes or until heated through.

6 TO 8 SERVINGS.

HARVARD BEETS

5 medium beets (about 1¼ pounds)
1 tablespoon cornstarch
1 tablespoon sugar
¾ teaspoon salt
Dash of pepper
⅔ cup water
¼ cup vinegar

Cook beets until tender, 35 to 45 minutes. Drain and cool slightly. Slip off skins and cut into slices.

Mix cornstarch, sugar, salt and pepper in a small saucepan. Gradually stir in water and vinegar. Cook, stirring constantly, until the mixture thickens and boils. Boil and stir 1 minute. Stir in the beets and heat through.

4 SERVINGS.

CHIVE-BUTTERED CARROTS

1½ pounds carrots or 2 cans (16 ounces each) whole carrots, drained
¼ cup butter or margarine
¼ teaspoon seasoned salt
⅛ teaspoon pepper
1 tablespoon snipped chives or minced onion

If using fresh carrots, cook until tender, 20 to 25 minutes; drain.

Melt butter in a large skillet and add carrots. Sprinkle with salt, pepper and chives. Heat through, turning carrots occasionally to coat with butter.

5 OR 6 SERVINGS.

GOLDEN CORN PUDDING

1 can (16 ounces) whole kernel corn, drained (about 2 cups)
1 teaspoon sugar
1 teaspoon salt
⅛ teaspoon pepper
2 eggs, well beaten
1 cup milk
1 tablespoon butter or margarine, melted
2 tablespoons cracker crumbs
2 tablespoons chopped green pepper
1 teaspoon chopped pimiento

Heat oven to 350°. Mix all ingredients thoroughly and pour into a greased 1-quart casserole. Place the casserole in a baking pan. Pour very hot water into the pan—to a depth of about 1 inch. Bake 50 to 60 minutes or until a knife inserted 1 inch from the edge of the casserole comes out clean. (The center will be soft but will set.)

6 SERVINGS.

DELUXE CREAMED ONIONS

2 pounds small white onions
   or 2 cans (16 ounces each)
   whole onions
2 tablespoons butter or margarine
2 tablespoons flour
½ teaspoon salt
⅛ teaspoon pepper
1½ cups light cream (20%)
1½ cups shredded carrots

If using fresh onions, peel and cook until tender, 15 to 20 minutes; drain. If using canned onions, simply heat and drain.

Melt butter in a large saucepan over low heat. Blend in flour and seasonings. Cook over low heat, stirring until the mixture is smooth and bubbly. Immediately stir in light cream. Heat to boiling, stirring constantly. Boil and stir 1 minute. Stir in carrots and cook about 5 minutes longer. Pour the sauce over the hot onions.

6 SERVINGS.

CLOVED ONIONS

1½ pounds small white onions
   or 1 can (16 ounces) whole
   onions, drained
3 tablespoons butter or margarine
⅛ teaspoon cloves
⅓ cup brown sugar (packed)

If using fresh onions, peel and cook until tender, 15 to 20 minutes; drain.

Melt butter with cloves in a large skillet over medium heat, stirring occasionally. Add onions and stir gently until coated. Sprinkle brown sugar over onions; cook, turning frequently, about 5 minutes—until onions are golden and glazed.

4 SERVINGS.

SPINACH GOURMET

1 pound fresh spinach or 1
   package (10 ounces) frozen
   chopped spinach
1 jar (4½ ounces) button
   mushrooms, drained
1 teaspoon instant minced onion
1 small clove garlic, crushed
½ teaspoon salt
   Dash of pepper
⅓ cup dairy sour cream
1 tablespoon light cream or milk

Cook spinach until tender, 3 to 5 minutes; drain. Combine spinach, mushrooms and seasonings in a saucepan. Blend sour cream and light cream. Pour over the spinach mixture and heat just to boiling.

4 SERVINGS.

FRENCH FRIED ONION RINGS

1 large Spanish or Bermuda
  onion
⅔ cup milk
½ cup all-purpose flour*
¾ teaspoon baking powder
¼ teaspoon salt

*If using self-rising flour, omit baking powder and salt.

Cut the onion into ¼-inch slices and separate into rings. In a large skillet, heat fat or oil (1 inch deep) to 375°. (The fat is hot enough if a 1-inch cube of bread browns in 60 seconds.) Beat the remaining ingredients until smooth.

Dip onion rings into the batter and let the excess batter drip back into the bowl. Fry a few onion rings at a time until golden brown, about 2 minutes. Turn only once. Drain. Serve hot.

3 OR 4 SERVINGS.

Note: To keep warm, place in 300° oven until ready to serve. Or make them several hours ahead of time and heat 7 to 10 minutes.

ZUCCHINI PROVENÇALE

4 small zucchini (about 1 pound)
1 onion, thinly sliced
½ cup finely chopped green pepper
2 tablespoons salad oil
1 clove garlic, crushed
1 teaspoon salt
⅛ teaspoon pepper
2 tomatoes, peeled and cut
  into wedges
  Snipped parsley
  Grated Parmesan cheese

Cut the unpared zucchini into ¼-inch slices (about 2 cups). Cook and stir all ingredients except the tomato wedges, parsley and cheese in a medium skillet until heated through. Cover and cook over medium heat, stirring occasionally, until the vegetables are crisp-tender, about 5 minutes.

Add tomato wedges. Cover and cook over low heat just until tomatoes are heated through, about 3 minutes. Sprinkle with parsley and cheese.

4 SERVINGS.

Breads

Breads

Homemade bread is many things to many people. A nostalgic memory. A heavenly aroma. An unforgettable taste experience. A gift of love in a bread basket. And to the baker goes the satisfaction of setting the stage for all these good things.

During our years of countless bakings, we've collected recipes for all kinds of breads and recipes for all kinds of bread bakers. And for this chapter, we've chosen to share those that represent the many favorites, both yours and ours. Some of these, like the classic White Bread and Bohemian Braid, start with yeast doughs that you knead and push and slap to a satiny elasticity. (Good tension-relieving therapy, we say.) Mixer-blended yeast batters let you hasten the pace a bit for Easy Oatmeal Bread or Dill Batter Buns. Then, too, there are the speedier-still baking powder breads, such as Sour Cream Coffee Cake, Pumpkin Bread and Southern Buttermilk Biscuits.

Of course, we've included our own specialties. Like our recipe for Popovers, with the built-in tips that guarantee showy, puffy perfection—every time. And the one for Buttermilk Herb Bread, which combines baking powder *and* yeast to speed up the rising. Potato Refrigerator Rolls were developed so you could have a dough to keep on hand, to shape and bake at any time. Stir 'n Roll Biscuits, a particularly happy innovation, call for oil instead of shortening and feature a streamlined method. Memorable, too, are Quick Corn Bread and Chive Dinner Muffins, recipes with shortcut ways to homemade flavor.

So why wait? Shape a dough or pour a batter. Find out about all the nice things that happen when you bake your own breads.

On the preceding pages:
Cinnamon Whirligig,
Pumpernickel Bread,
Pumpkin Bread,
French Breakfast Puffs,
Rich Egg Braid,
Southern Buttermilk Biscuits
   and Golden Crescents

WHITE BREAD

2 packages active dry yeast
¾ cup warm water (105 to 115°)
2⅔ cups warm water
¼ cup sugar
1 tablespoon salt
3 tablespoons shortening
9 to 10 cups all-purpose flour*
Soft butter, margarine or
shortening

*If using self-rising flour, omit salt.

The homemaker of old had no alternative but to bake at least 12 to 14 loaves each week. These days, we don't *have* to make bread—we *choose* to. And that seems like a much happier, more satisfying way to go about it.

So whether you're starting on your first loaf or your fifty-first, here are some technique tips for perfect yeast breads:

1. Make sure the water is 105 to 115°. A thermometer is the best guide. If you don't have one, test a drop of water on the inside of your wrist—the water should feel very warm but not hot.

2. Let the dough rise in a warm, draft-free place. If necessary, set the bowl of dough on a wire rack over a bowl of warm water.

3. To test the raised dough for doubled bulk, press two fingers about ½ inch into the raised dough. If the dough has doubled, the impressions will remain.

Dissolve yeast in ¾ cup warm water. Stir in 2⅔ cups water, the sugar, salt, shortening and 4½ cups of the flour. Beat until smooth. Mix in enough of the remaining flour (first with a spoon and then by hand) to make the dough easy to handle.

Turn the dough onto a lightly floured board and knead until smooth and elastic, about 10 minutes. Place in a greased bowl; turn the greased side up. Cover and let rise in a warm place until double, about 1 hour. (The dough is ready if an indentation remains when touched.)

Punch down the dough and divide in half. Roll each half into a rectangle, 18×9 inches. Roll up, beginning at the short side. With the side of your hand, press down on each end to seal; fold under loaf. Place seam side down in a greased loaf pan, 9×5×3 inches. Brush the loaves with butter. Let rise until double, about 1 hour.

Heat oven to 425°. Place loaves on a low rack so that the tops of the pans are level with or slightly above the center of the oven. For even browning, the pans should not touch each other or the sides of the oven. Bake 30 to 35 minutes or until the loaves are a deep golden brown and sound hollow when tapped. (If the loaves are browning too quickly, cover with foil for the last 15 minutes of baking.) Immediately remove from the pans and cool on a wire rack. For a soft, shiny crust, brush the hot loaves with butter or shortening.

2 LOAVES.

Note: Three loaf pans, 8½×4½×2½ inches, can be used. Divide the dough into 3 equal parts after punching it down.

2 packages active dry yeast
½ cup warm water (105 to 115°)
1½ cups lukewarm milk (scalded
   then cooled)
¼ cup sugar
1 tablespoon salt
3 eggs
¼ cup shortening or butter
   or margarine, softened
7¼ to 7½ cups all-purpose flour*
2 cups raisins

*If using self-rising flour, omit salt.

A tender, rich, yellow-yummy
bread—thanks to the eggs—that
makes just about the best toast
ever. A "rather not" on the raisins?
Forget about them. You'll find
you've made our equally well-
known Rich Egg Bread.

NEW ENGLAND RAISIN BREAD

Dissolve yeast in warm water. Stir in milk, sugar, salt, eggs, shortening and about 3½ cups of the flour. Beat until smooth. Mix in raisins and enough of the remaining flour to make the dough easy to handle.

Turn the dough onto a lightly floured board and knead until smooth and elastic, about 5 minutes. Place in a greased bowl; turn the greased side up. Cover and let rise in a warm place until double, 1½ to 2 hours.

Punch down the dough and divide in half. Roll each half into a rectangle, 18×9 inches. Roll up, beginning at the short side. With the side of your hand, press down on each end to seal; fold under loaf. Place seam side down in a greased loaf pan, 9×5×3 or 8½×4½×2½ inches. Let rise until double, about 1 hour.

Heat oven to 400°. Bake on low rack 25 to 30 minutes or until the loaves are golden brown and sound hollow when tapped. Immediately remove from the pans and cool. Brush with butter or shortening or frost with Creamy Icing (page 73).

2 LOAVES.

VARIATION

Rich Egg Braid: Omit raisins. After punching down dough, divide into thirds. Divide each third into 3 equal parts; shape each into a strand, about 14 inches long. Loosely braid each group of 3 strands on a greased baking sheet. Pinch ends and tuck under. Brush with butter. Cover and let rise until double, 40 to 50 minutes. Mix 1 egg yolk and 2 tablespoons cold water; brush on braid. Heat oven to 375°. Bake 25 to 30 minutes. 3 BRAIDS.

BUTTERMILK HERB BREAD

2 packages active dry yeast
¾ cup warm water (105 to 115°)
2 teaspoons caraway seed
½ teaspoon crumbled leaf sage
½ teaspoon nutmeg
1¼ cups buttermilk
4½ to 5 cups all-purpose flour*
¼ cup shortening
2 tablespoons sugar
2 teaspoons baking powder
2 teaspoons salt
  Soft butter or margarine

*If using self-rising flour, omit baking powder and salt.

A timesaving yeast bread? This one was developed especially for the electric mixer. And it requires only one rising! So why not make two of these "can-do-quick" loaves while you're at it. Just double all ingredients except the yeast. Blend 1 minute on low speed, scraping the bowl constantly. Beat 4 minutes on medium speed, scraping occasionally. Then stir in the remaining flour. Knead, divide the dough in half and shape into two loaves.

Grease a loaf pan, 9×5×3 inches. Dissolve yeast in warm water in a large mixer bowl. Stir in caraway seed, sage and nutmeg. Add buttermilk, 2½ cups of the flour, the shortening, sugar, baking powder and salt. Blend ½ minute on low speed, scraping the bowl constantly. Beat 2 minutes on medium speed, scraping occasionally. Stir in the remaining flour. (The dough should remain soft and slightly sticky.)

Turn the dough onto a well-floured board and knead until smooth, about 5 minutes. Roll the dough into a rectangle, 18×9 inches. Roll up, beginning at the short side. With the side of your hand, press down on each end to seal; fold under loaf. Place seam side down in the pan. Brush the loaf lightly with butter. Let rise in a warm place until double, about 1 hour. (The dough in the center should be about 2 inches above the pan.)

Heat oven to 425°. Place the oven rack in the lowest position or bread will brown too quickly. Bake 30 to 35 minutes. (If the loaf is browning too quickly, cover with foil for the last 15 minutes of baking.) Immediately remove from the pan and cool on a wire rack. For a soft, shiny crust, brush the top with butter or shortening.

VARIATIONS

Garlic Bread: Omit caraway seed, leaf sage and nutmeg and add ¾ teaspoon garlic powder.

Whole Wheat Bread: Omit caraway seed, leaf sage and nutmeg. Substitute 1½ cups all-purpose flour and 1 cup whole wheat flour for the first addition of flour; substitute 2 cups whole wheat flour for the second addition of flour.

¾ **cup boiling water**
½ **cup oats**
3 **tablespoons shortening**
¼ **cup light molasses**
2 **teaspoons salt**
1 **package active dry yeast**
¼ **cup warm water (105 to 115°)**
1 **egg**
2¾ **cups all-purpose flour***

*If using self-rising flour, omit salt.

Batter breads like these are shortcut yeast breads. They require no kneading or shaping so they're easier to make and take about half the time. You simply mix the ingredients with an electric mixer and spread the batter evenly in the pan. (Batter breads have a more open texture than kneaded breads, but they're very moist and tender.)

A word of caution: Too much rising will cause the loaf to collapse. If the dough should rise too high in the pan, simply remove it, punch it down and let it rise again.

EASY OATMEAL BREAD

Grease a loaf pan, 9 × 5 × 3 or 8½ × 4½ × 2½ inches. Combine boiling water, oats, shortening, molasses and salt in a large mixer bowl. Cool to lukewarm.

Dissolve yeast in warm water. Add yeast, egg and 1½ cups of the flour to the oat mixture. Beat 2 minutes on medium speed, scraping the bowl frequently. Stir in the remaining flour until smooth.

Spread the batter evenly in the pan. The batter will be sticky—smooth and pat into shape with floured hands. Let rise in a warm place until the batter is 1 inch from the top of the 9-inch pan or reaches the top of the 8½-inch pan, about 1½ hours.

Heat oven to 375°. Bake 50 to 55 minutes or until the loaf is brown and sounds hollow when tapped. (If the loaf is browning too quickly, cover with foil for the last 15 minutes of baking.) Remove from the pan and cool on a wire rack. For a soft, shiny crust, brush the top with butter or shortening.

VARIATIONS

Anadama Batter Bread: Substitute ½ cup yellow cornmeal for the oats.

Little Loaves: Grease 6 miniature loaf pans, 4½ × 2½ × 1½ inches. Divide the batter among the pans and let rise until it just reaches the tops of the pans, about 1½ hours. Bake 35 to 40 minutes.

SWEDISH LIMPA RYE BREAD

2 packages active dry yeast
1½ cups warm water (105 to 115°)
¼ cup molasses
⅓ cup sugar
1 tablespoon salt
2 tablespoons shortening
  Grated peel of 1 to 2 oranges
2½ cups medium rye flour
2¼ to 2¾ cups all-purpose flour*
  Cornmeal

*If using self-rising flour, omit salt.

Dissolve yeast in warm water. Stir in molasses, sugar, salt, shortening, orange peel and rye flour. Beat until smooth. Mix in enough of the white flour to make the dough easy to handle.

Turn the dough onto a lightly floured board. Cover and let rest 10 to 15 minutes. Knead until smooth, about 5 minutes. Place in a greased bowl; turn the greased side up. Cover and let rise in a warm place until double, about 1 hour. (The dough is ready if an indentation remains when touched.)

Punch down the dough; round up, cover and let rise until double, about 40 minutes.

Grease a baking sheet and sprinkle with cornmeal. Punch down the dough and divide in half. Shape each half into a slightly flattened round loaf. Place the loaves in opposite corners of the baking sheet. Cover and let rise 1 hour.

Heat oven to 375°. Bake 30 to 35 minutes. Cool on a wire rack.

2 LOAVES.

PUMPERNICKEL BREAD

3 packages active dry yeast
1½ cups warm water (105 to 115°)
½ cup molasses
3 teaspoons salt
2 tablespoons shortening
2 tablespoons caraway seed
2¾ cups rye flour
2¼ to 2¾ cups all-purpose flour*
  Cornmeal

*If using self-rising flour, omit salt.

Dissolve yeast in warm water. Stir in molasses, salt, shortening, caraway seed and rye flour. Beat until smooth. Mix in enough of the white flour to make the dough easy to handle.

Knead and shape as directed for Swedish Limpa Rye Bread (above). Bake 25 to 30 minutes.

2 LOAVES.

POTATO REFRIGERATOR ROLLS

1 package active dry yeast
1½ cups warm water (105 to 115°)
⅔ cup sugar
1½ teaspoons salt
⅔ cup shortening
2 eggs
1 cup lukewarm mashed potatoes
7 to 7½ cups all-purpose flour*
Soft butter or margarine

*If using self-rising flour, omit salt.

Dissolve yeast in warm water. Stir in sugar, salt, shortening, eggs, potatoes and 4 cups of the flour. Beat until smooth. Mix in enough of the remaining flour to make the dough easy to handle.

Turn the dough onto a lightly floured board and knead until smooth and elastic, about 5 minutes. Place in a greased bowl; turn the greased side up. Cover bowl tightly and refrigerate until ready to use. (The dough can be refrigerated at 45° or below for up to 5 days. Keep covered.) If the dough rises, punch it down occasionally.

When you want to make fresh rolls, punch down the dough and cut off the amount needed. Use ¼ of the dough for each of the shapes below. Shape, cover and let rise in a warm place until double, about 1½ hours.

Heat oven to 400°. Bake rolls 15 to 25 minutes.

Cloverleaf: Shape bits of dough into 1-inch balls. Place 3 balls in each greased medium muffin cup. Brush with butter. ABOUT 12 ROLLS.

Cobblestone: Shape bits of dough into 1½-inch balls. Place in a lightly greased layer pan, 9 × 1½ inches. Brush with butter. 2 DOZEN ROLLS.

Four-leaf Clover: Shape pieces of dough into 2-inch balls. Place each ball in a greased medium muffin cup. With scissors, snip each ball in half, then into quarters. Brush with butter. ABOUT 12 ROLLS.

Parker House: Roll dough into a rectangle, 13 × 9 inches, and cut into 3-inch circles. Brush with butter. Fold so the top half overlaps slightly. Press the edges together. Place on a lightly greased baking sheet. Brush with butter. ABOUT 10 ROLLS.

You can't beat the fragrance and flavor of homemade rolls. And with this do-ahead, keep-on-hand dough, you can boast hot-from-the-oven rolls on even your busiest days.

1. For quick Four-leaf Clovers, just snip each ball in half and then in half again.

2. For Parker House rolls, fold the circles slightly off-center to make sure the top half overlaps.

GOLDEN CRESCENTS

2 packages active dry yeast
¾ cup warm water (105 to 115°)
½ cup sugar
1 teaspoon salt
2 eggs
½ cup shortening (part soft butter)
4 cups all-purpose flour*
  Soft butter or margarine

*If using self-rising flour, omit salt.

Dissolve yeast in warm water. Stir in sugar, salt, eggs, shortening and 2 cups of the flour. Beat until smooth. Gradually mix in the remaining flour until smooth. Cover and let rise in a warm place until double, about 1½ hours. (The dough is ready if an indentation remains when touched.)

Divide the dough in half and roll each half into a 12-inch circle. Brush with butter and cut into 16 wedges. Roll up each wedge, beginning at the rounded edge. Place the rolls with points under on a greased baking sheet. Cover and let rise until double, about 1 hour.

Heat oven to 400°. Bake 12 to 15 minutes or until golden brown. Brush the rolls with butter.

32 ROLLS.

QUICK SOUR CREAM ROLLS

2 packages active dry yeast
¾ cup warm water (105 to 115°)
¾ cup buttermilk
¾ cup dairy sour cream
5½ cups all-purpose flour*
½ cup shortening
2 tablespoons sugar
2 teaspoons baking powder
2 teaspoons salt

*If using self-rising flour, omit baking powder and salt.

Dissolve yeast in warm water in a large mixer bowl. Add buttermilk, sour cream, 2½ cups of the flour, the shortening, sugar, baking powder and salt. Blend ½ minute on low speed, scraping the bowl constantly. Beat 2 minutes on medium speed, scraping occasionally. Stir in the remaining flour.

Turn the dough onto a well-floured board and knead until smooth, about 5 minutes. Divide the dough in 3 equal parts. Use one third to shape any of the rolls on page 60. Let rise 1 hour.

Heat oven to 375°. Bake 20 to 25 minutes or until golden brown.

ABOUT 3 DOZEN ROLLS.

BRAN PAN BISCUITS

1 package active dry yeast
1 cup warm water (105 to 115°)
¼ cup brown sugar (packed)
1½ teaspoons salt
½ cup whole bran or oats
1 egg
3 tablespoons shortening
3½ to 3¾ cups all-purpose flour*

*If using self-rising flour, omit salt.

Dissolve yeast in warm water. Stir in sugar, salt, bran, egg, shortening and 1¾ cups of the flour. Beat until smooth. Mix in enough of the remaining flour to make the dough easy to handle.

Place the dough in a greased bowl; turn the greased side up. Cover and let rise in a warm place until double, about 1½ hours. (The dough is ready if an indentation remains when touched.)

Punch down the dough and, with greased hands, shape into 1½-inch balls. (The dough will be slightly sticky.) Place in 2 greased layer pans, 9 × 1½ inches. Cover and let rise until double, about 45 minutes.

Heat oven to 375°. Bake 20 to 25 minutes.

2 DOZEN BISCUITS.

DILL BATTER BUNS

¾ cup dairy sour cream
1 package active dry yeast
¼ cup warm water (105 to 115°)
2 tablespoons sugar
1 teaspoon salt
2 tablespoons shortening
1 egg
1½ tablespoons fresh dill
    seed or snipped chives
2¼ cups all-purpose flour*

*If using self-rising flour, omit salt.

Heat sour cream *just* to lukewarm. Dissolve yeast in warm water. Stir in sour cream, sugar, salt, shortening, egg, dill seed and about 1½ cups of the flour. Beat until smooth. Stir in the remaining flour until smooth. Cover and let rise in a warm place until double, about 30 minutes.

Grease 16 medium muffin cups. Stir down the batter and fill the cups ½ full. (The batter will be sticky—smooth and pat into shape with floured fingers.) Let rise until the dough reaches the tops of the muffin cups, 20 to 30 minutes.

Heat oven to 400°. Bake 15 to 20 minutes or until golden brown.

16 BUNS.

SOUTHERN BUTTERMILK BISCUITS

2 cups all-purpose flour*
2 teaspoons sugar
2 teaspoons baking powder
1 teaspoon salt
½ teaspoon soda
⅓ cup shortening
⅔ cup buttermilk

*If using self-rising flour, omit baking powder and salt.

Heat oven to 450°. Measure flour, sugar, baking powder, salt and soda into a bowl. Cut in shortening with a pastry blender until the mixture looks like meal. Stir in almost all the buttermilk until the mixture rounds up into a ball and no dry ingredients remain in the bowl. If the dough is not pliable, add just enough milk to make a soft, puffy, easy-to-roll dough. (Too much milk will make the dough sticky, too little will make the biscuits dry.)

Round up the dough on a lightly floured cloth-covered board and knead lightly 20 to 25 times, about ½ minute. Roll a little less than ½ inch thick and cut with a floured biscuit cutter. Place on an ungreased baking sheet. For crusty sides, place them 1 inch apart; for soft sides, place them close together in an ungreased layer pan. Bake 10 to 12 minutes or until golden brown. Serve hot, with butter and, if you like, honey or jam.

ABOUT 2 DOZEN 1¾-INCH BISCUITS.

CHIVE DINNER MUFFINS

2 cups buttermilk baking mix
2 tablespoons shortening
1 egg
⅔ cup milk or water
¼ cup snipped chives

Heat oven to 400°. Grease 12 medium muffin cups. Mix all ingredients with a fork and beat vigorously ½ minute. Fill the muffin cups ⅔ full. Bake 12 to 15 minutes or until light brown.

12 MUFFINS.

VARIATION

Herb Dinner Muffins: Omit chives and add 1¼ teaspoons caraway seed, ½ teaspoon crumbled leaf sage and ¼ teaspoon nutmeg.

STIR 'N ROLL BISCUITS

2 cups all-purpose flour*
3 teaspoons baking powder
1 teaspoon salt
⅓ cup salad oil
⅔ cup milk

*If using self-rising flour, omit baking powder and salt.

Heat oven to 450°. Measure flour, baking powder and salt into a bowl. Pour oil and milk into a measuring cup (do not stir together) and pour all at once into the dry ingredients. Stir with a fork just until the mixture cleans the side of the bowl and rounds up into a ball.

To knead the dough, turn onto waxed paper. Lift up one corner of the paper and fold the dough in half, pressing paper down firmly on the dough. Pull paper back and repeat until the dough looks smooth (about 10 times).

Pat or roll ½ inch thick between 2 sheets of waxed paper and cut with an unfloured biscuit cutter. Place on an ungreased baking sheet. Bake 10 to 12 minutes or until golden brown. Serve hot.

ABOUT SIXTEEN 1¾-INCH BISCUITS.

WHOLE WHEAT MUFFINS

1 egg
1 cup milk
¼ cup salad oil
1 cup all-purpose flour*
1 cup whole wheat flour
¼ cup sugar
2 teaspoons baking powder
1 teaspoon salt

*If using self-rising flour, omit baking powder and salt.

Heat oven to 400°. Grease the bottoms of 12 medium muffin cups. Beat egg and stir in milk and oil. Mix in the remaining ingredients just until the flour is moistened. The batter should be lumpy. Fill the muffin cups ⅔ full. Bake 20 to 25 minutes or until golden brown. Serve hot.

12 MUFFINS.

¼ **cup butter or margarine**
1¼ **cups all-purpose flour***
 2 **teaspoons sugar**
 2 **teaspoons baking powder**
 1 **teaspoon salt**
 ⅔ **cup milk**

*If using self-rising flour, omit baking powder and salt.

Change the flavor and give snappy savor to these delectable dips by simply adding ½ clove garlic, very finely minced, to the melted butter. Or sprinkle the butter-coated strips with salt, garlic salt or caraway seed.

BUTTER DIPS

Heat oven to 450°. Melt butter in the oven in a baking pan, 9×9×2 inches. Remove pan from oven.

Measure flour, sugar, baking powder and salt into a bowl. Add milk and stir with a fork just until the dough forms a ball, about 30 strokes.

Turn the dough onto a well-floured cloth-covered board. Roll dough around several times to coat with flour. Knead lightly about 10 times and roll into an 8-inch square. With a floured knife, cut the dough in half, then cut each half into 9 strips.

Dip each strip into the melted butter, coating both sides. Arrange the strips close together in 2 rows in the pan. Bake 15 to 20 minutes or until golden brown. Serve hot.

18 STICKS.

VARIATION

Cheese Butter Dips: Add ½ cup shredded sharp American cheese to the dry ingredients.

GARLIC BISCUIT BREAD

Heat oven to 450°. Prepare Biscuit dough as directed on a package of buttermilk baking mix except—do not knead.

On a greased baking sheet, spread or roll the dough into a rectangle, 10×8 inches. Brush 1 tablespoon soft butter or margarine on the dough and sprinkle with garlic salt. Bake 10 minutes. Serve hot, broken into pieces or cut into squares.

6 SERVINGS.

QUICK CORN BREAD

1¼ cups buttermilk baking mix
¾ cup cornmeal
2 tablespoons sugar
½ teaspoon salt
1 egg
2 tablespoons shortening
⅔ cup milk

Heat oven to 400°. Grease a baking pan, 8 × 8 × 2 inches. Mix all ingredients with a spoon and beat vigorously ½ minute. Spread in the pan. Bake 20 to 25 minutes. Serve warm.

8 SERVINGS.

POPOVERS

2 eggs
1 cup milk
1 cup all-purpose flour*
½ teaspoon salt

*Do not use self-rising flour in this recipe.

Heat oven to 450°. Grease 6 deep custard cups or 8 medium muffin cups. With a rotary beater, beat eggs slightly. Add the remaining ingredients and beat just until smooth. *Do not overbeat.*

Fill the custard cups ½ full, muffin cups ¾ full. Bake 25 minutes, then reduce oven temperature to 350° and bake 15 to 20 minutes longer or until a deep golden brown. Immediately remove from cups.

6 TO 8 POPOVERS.

Three pointers to help you get high-as-the-sky popovers like these every time: **1.** Don't overbeat the batter. **2.** Make sure the oven temperature is on target. **3.** Use deep custard cups for a really spectacular pop-up.

BUTTERSCOTCH-PECAN ROLLS

1 package active dry yeast
¼ cup warm water (105 to 115°)
¼ cup lukewarm milk (scalded then cooled)
¼ cup granulated sugar
½ teaspoon salt
1 egg
¼ cup shortening
2¼ to 2½ cups all-purpose flour*
½ cup butter or margarine
½ cup brown sugar (packed)
½ cup pecan halves
2 tablespoons soft butter or margarine
¼ cup granulated sugar
2 teaspoons cinnamon

*If using self-rising flour, omit salt.

Learn the ABC's of this adaptable, rich sweet roll dough. From it you can create any number of coffee cakes as well as a kaleidoscope of rolls in all shapes and sizes. We used it to make the Swedish Tea Ring on page 75 and the Hungarian Coffee Cake on page 76.

Dissolve yeast in warm water. Stir in milk, ¼ cup granulated sugar, the salt, egg, shortening and 1½ cups of the flour. Beat until smooth. Mix in enough of the remaining flour to make the dough easy to handle.

Turn the dough onto a lightly floured board and knead until smooth and elastic, about 5 minutes. Place in a greased bowl; turn the greased side up. (At this point, the dough can be covered and refrigerated at 45° or below for up to 4 days.) Cover and let rise in a warm place until double, about 1½ hours. (The dough is ready if an indentation remains when touched.)

Melt ½ cup butter in a baking pan, 13×9×2 inches. Sprinkle brown sugar and pecan halves over the butter.

Punch down the dough and roll into a rectangle, 15×9 inches. Spread with 2 tablespoons butter. Mix ¼ cup granulated sugar and the cinnamon and sprinkle over the rectangle. Roll up tightly, beginning at the wide side. Pinch the edge of the dough into the roll to seal well; stretch the roll to make even. Cut into 1-inch slices and place slightly apart in the pan. Cover and let rise until double, about 45 minutes.

Heat oven to 375°. Bake 25 to 30 minutes. Immediately invert the pan onto a serving plate. Let the pan remain a minute so the butterscotch can drizzle down over the rolls.

15 ROLLS.

FROSTED ORANGE ROLLS

Dough for Butterscotch-Pecan
Rolls (page 68)
3 tablespoons soft butter or
margarine
1 tablespoon grated orange peel
2 tablespoons orange juice
1½ cups confectioners' sugar

Prepare the dough for Butterscotch-Pecan Rolls. After punching down the dough, roll into a rectangle, 15×9 inches. Mix butter, orange peel, orange juice and sugar; spread half the mixture over the rectangle.

Roll up tightly, beginning at the wide side. Pinch the edge of the dough into the roll to seal well; stretch the roll to make even. Cut into 1-inch slices and place slightly apart in a well-greased baking pan, 13×9×2 inches. Cover and let rise until double, about 45 minutes.

Heat oven to 375°. Bake 25 to 30 minutes. While warm, top the rolls with the remaining orange mixture.

15 ROLLS.

FANCY FRUIT BUNS

1 package active dry yeast
¼ cup warm water (105 to 115°)
½ cup lukewarm milk (scalded
then cooled)
¼ cup sugar
1 teaspoon salt
¼ cup shortening
1 egg
2¼ cups all-purpose flour*
¼ teaspoon mace
½ teaspoon nutmeg
½ cup cut-up candied fruits
¼ cup raisins
¼ cup chopped nuts
Creamy Icing (page 73)

*If using self-rising flour, omit salt.

Dissolve yeast in warm water. Stir in milk, sugar, salt, shortening, egg and 1¼ cups of the flour. Beat until smooth. Mix in the remaining flour, the mace, nutmeg, fruits and nuts. Cover and let rise in a warm place until double, about 1¾ hours.

Beat down the dough and drop by tablespoonfuls about 3 inches apart onto a greased baking sheet. Let rise until double, about 30 minutes.

Heat oven to 400°. Bake about 15 minutes or until golden brown. While warm, drizzle buns with Creamy Icing.

1½ DOZEN BUNS.

1 cup dairy sour cream
1 package active dry yeast
¼ cup warm water (105 to 115°)
2 tablespoons butter or margarine, softened
3 tablespoons granulated sugar
1 teaspoon salt
1 egg
3 cups all-purpose flour*
2 tablespoons soft butter or margarine
⅓ cup brown sugar (packed)
1 teaspoon cinnamon
  Creamy Glaze (below)

*If using self-rising flour, omit salt.

As soon as you finish each twist, place it on the baking sheet. Gently press both ends to keep the proper shape.

SOUR CREAM TWISTS

Heat sour cream *just* to lukewarm. Dissolve yeast in warm water. Stir in sour cream, 2 tablespoons butter, the granulated sugar, salt, egg and 1 cup of the flour and beat until smooth. Mix in the remaining flour until the dough cleans the side of the bowl.

Turn the dough onto a lightly floured board and knead until smooth, about 10 minutes. Place in a greased bowl; turn the greased side up. Cover and let rise in a warm place until double, about 1 hour. (The dough is ready if an indentation remains when touched.)

Punch down the dough and roll into a rectangle, 24 × 6 inches. Brush with 2 tablespoons butter. Mix brown sugar and cinnamon and sprinkle over a lengthwise half of the rectangle. Fold the other half over the sugared half. Cut into 1-inch strips.

Holding the strips at each end, twist in opposite directions. Place 2 inches apart on a greased baking sheet, pressing the ends on the sheet. Cover and let rise until double, about 1 hour.

Heat oven to 375°. Bake 12 to 15 minutes or until golden brown. While warm, frost with Creamy Glaze.

2 DOZEN TWISTS.

CREAMY GLAZE

Mix 1½ cups confectioners' sugar, 2 tablespoons soft butter or margarine, 1½ teaspoons vanilla and 1 to 2 tablespoons hot water until smooth and of spreading consistency.

OVERNIGHT CINNAMON ROLLS

1 package active dry yeast
¼ cup warm water (105 to 115°)
4 cups all-purpose flour*
¼ cup sugar
1 teaspoon salt
1 cup butter or margarine, softened
3 egg yolks, beaten
1 cup lukewarm milk (scalded then cooled)
2 tablespoons butter or margarine, melted
½ cup sugar
1½ teaspoons cinnamon
Creamy Glaze (page 70)

*If using self-rising flour, omit salt.

Miniature pinwheel coffee cakes with a delightfully rich, buttery tenderness. Since well-chilled dough is essential for easy handling, these rolls (also called Danish Cinnamon Puffs) have a built-in do-ahead, keep-awhile advantage. Perfect for small families who want just a few at a time. They can save the rest of the dough for more fresh rolls, warm from the oven, a morning or two later.

Dissolve yeast in warm water. Mix flour, ¼ cup sugar and the salt in a large bowl. Cut in 1 cup butter with a pastry blender until the mixture looks like meal. Stir in yeast, egg yolks and milk. Mix until the dough is smooth. Cover and refrigerate at least 8 hours or until ready to use. (The dough can be refrigerated at 45° or below for up to 3 days. Keep covered.)

Grease 24 medium muffin cups. Turn half the dough onto a well-floured board and roll into a rectangle, 12 × 10 inches. Brush with 1 tablespoon melted butter. Mix ½ cup sugar and the cinnamon and sprinkle half the mixture over the rectangle. Roll up, beginning at the wide side. Pinch the edge of the dough into the roll to seal well; stretch the roll to make even. Cut into 1-inch slices and place in the muffin cups. Repeat with the remaining dough. Cover and let rise until double, 1 to 1½ hours.

Heat oven to 375°. Bake 15 to 20 minutes or until golden. While warm, frost rolls with Creamy Glaze.

2 DOZEN ROLLS.

Note: You can mix this dough with an electric mixer. Dissolve yeast in warm water in a large mixer bowl. Add ¼ cup sugar, the milk, egg yolks, salt, 1 cup butter and 2 cups of the flour. Blend ½ minute on low speed, scraping the bowl constantly. Beat 2 minutes on medium speed, scraping occasionally. With a spoon, stir in the remaining flour until the dough is smooth.

BALLOON BUNS

1 package active dry yeast
¼ cup warm water (105 to 115°)
¾ cup lukewarm milk (scalded then cooled)
¼ cup sugar
1 teaspoon salt
1 egg
¼ cup shortening
3½ to 3¾ cups all-purpose flour*
1 cup sugar
1 tablespoon cinnamon
18 large marshmallows
½ cup butter or margarine, melted

*If using self-rising flour, omit salt.

Marshmallows do such magic things to these sweet rolls that it's easy to understand why we first called them Hocus Pocus Buns. A marshmallow starts out in the middle and, presto, it disappears— melting away to a sugar 'n spice hollow. A treat that's well worth the trick!

Dissolve yeast in warm water. Stir in milk, ¼ cup sugar, the salt, egg, shortening and 1¾ cups of the flour. Beat until smooth. Mix in enough of the remaining flour to make the dough easy to handle.

Turn the dough onto a lightly floured board and knead until smooth and elastic, about 5 minutes. Place in a greased bowl; turn the greased side up. Cover and let rise in a warm place until double, about 1½ hours. (The dough is ready if an indentation remains when touched.)

Punch down the dough and divide in half. Roll each half about ¼ inch thick and cut into nine 3½-inch circles. Mix 1 cup sugar and the cinnamon in a small bowl. Dip each marshmallow into the melted butter, then into the sugar-cinnamon mixture. Wrap a circle of dough around each marshmallow, pinching together tightly at the bottom. Dip in the butter, then in the sugar-cinnamon mixture. Place in greased medium muffin cups. Let rise about 20 minutes.

Heat oven to 375°. Bake 25 to 30 minutes. Serve warm.

1½ DOZEN ROLLS.

CHOCOLATE CINNAMON ROLLS

1 package active dry yeast
¼ cup warm water (105 to 115°)
¼ cup lukewarm milk (scalded then cooled)
¼ cup sugar
½ teaspoon salt
1 egg
¼ cup shortening
⅓ cup cocoa
2¼ to 2½ cups all-purpose flour*
2 tablespoons soft butter or margarine
¼ cup sugar
1½ teaspoons cinnamon
Creamy Icing (below)

*If using self-rising flour, omit salt.

Dissolve yeast in warm water. Stir in milk, ¼ cup sugar, the salt, egg, shortening, cocoa and 1½ cups of the flour. Beat until smooth. Mix in enough of the remaining flour to make the dough easy to handle.

Turn the dough onto a lightly floured board and knead until smooth and elastic, about 5 minutes. Place in a greased bowl; turn the greased side up. (At this point, the dough can be covered and refrigerated at 45° or below for up to 4 days.) Cover and let rise in a warm place until double, about 1½ hours. (The dough is ready if an indentation remains when touched.)

Punch down the dough and roll into a rectangle, 15 × 9 inches. Spread with butter. Mix ¼ cup sugar and the cinnamon and sprinkle over the rectangle. Roll up, beginning at the wide side. Pinch the edge of the dough into the roll to seal well; stretch the roll to make even. Cut into 1-inch slices and place slightly apart in a greased baking pan, 13 × 9 × 2 inches. Let rise until double, about 45 minutes.

Heat oven to 375°. Bake 25 to 30 minutes. While warm, frost rolls with Creamy Icing.

15 ROLLS.

CREAMY ICING

Mix ¾ cup confectioners' sugar, 1½ teaspoons milk and ¼ teaspoon vanilla until smooth.

CINNAMON WHIRLIGIG

Dough for Balloon Buns
(page 72)
¼ cup sugar
2 teaspoons cinnamon

Prepare the dough for Balloon Buns. After punching down the dough, roll into a rectangle, 16 × 8 inches. Mix sugar and cinnamon and sprinkle over the rectangle.

Roll up tightly, beginning at the narrow side. Pinch the edge of the dough into the roll to seal well. Place seam side down in a well-greased loaf pan, 9 × 5 × 3 inches. Let rise until double, about 1 hour.

Heat oven to 375°. Bake 35 minutes or until golden brown. If the loaf is browning too quickly, cover with foil for the last 15 minutes of baking. For a soft, shiny crust, brush the top of the still-hot loaf with butter or shortening; or you can frost the cooled loaf with Creamy Icing (page 73).

HUNGARIAN COFFEE CAKE

Double recipe for Butterscotch-
Pecan Rolls dough (page 68)
¾ cup sugar
1 teaspoon cinnamon
½ cup finely chopped nuts
½ cup butter or margarine, melted

Prepare the double recipe of dough. After punching down the dough, shape pieces into 1½-inch balls. Mix sugar, cinnamon and nuts in a small bowl. Dip balls in melted butter, then roll in the sugar-cinnamon-nut mixture.

Place a single layer of balls with sides just touching in a well-greased 10-inch tube pan. (If the pan has a removable bottom, line with aluminum foil.) Top with another layer of balls. Let rise until double, about 45 minutes.

Heat oven to 375°. Bake 35 to 40 minutes. (If the top is browning too quickly, cover with foil.) Loosen from pan and immediately invert the pan onto a serving plate. Let the pan remain a minute so the butter-sugar mixture can drizzle down over the coffee cake. To serve, break apart with 2 forks.

Hungarian Coffee Cake

Almond Topping (below)
1 package active dry yeast
¾ cup warm water (105 to 115°)
¼ cup sugar
1 teaspoon salt
1 egg
¼ cup shortening
2¼ cups all-purpose flour*

*If using self-rising flour, omit salt.

A one-bowl-for-everything coffee cake with the alias "Double Quick Coffee Bread." And an appropriate alias it is—beating takes the place of kneading, and no rolling or cutting is necessary. It's fluffier, thinner crusted and more cake-like in texture than its kneaded counterparts.

BUTTER ALMOND COFFEE CAKE

Prepare the topping. Dissolve yeast in warm water in a large mixer bowl. Add sugar, salt, egg, shortening and 1¼ cups of the flour. Beat 2 minutes on medium speed, scraping the bowl frequently. Mix in the remaining flour until smooth.

Drop the batter by tablespoonfuls onto the Almond Topping in the pan. Cover and let rise in a warm place until double, about 1 hour.

Heat oven to 375°. Bake 30 to 35 minutes or until golden brown. Immediately invert the pan onto a serving plate. Let the pan remain a minute so the topping can drizzle down over the coffee cake.

ALMOND TOPPING

Melt ⅓ cup butter in a baking pan, 9×9×2 inches. Stir in ½ cup slivered blanched almonds. Heat until the butter foams and the nuts are golden brown. Remove from heat and cool. Stir in 2 tablespoons light corn syrup, ½ cup sugar and ½ teaspoon almond extract. Spread the mixture evenly in the pan.

VARIATION

Butterscotch-Pecan Coffee Cake: Omit Almond Topping. Instead, melt ⅓ cup butter or margarine and ½ cup brown sugar (packed) with 1 tablespoon corn syrup in the baking pan. Sprinkle ½ cup pecans on mixture. (Candied or maraschino cherries can be added, too.) Cool.

SWEDISH TEA RING

Dough for Butterscotch-Pecan Rolls (page 68)
2 tablespoons soft butter or margarine
½ cup brown sugar (packed)
2 teaspoons cinnamon
½ cup raisins
Confectioners' Sugar Icing (page 78)
Walnuts
Candied cherry halves

Prepare the dough for Butterscotch-Pecan Rolls. After punching down the dough, roll into a rectangle, 15×9 inches. Spread with butter, then sprinkle with sugar, cinnamon and raisins. Roll up tightly, beginning at the wide side. Pinch the edge of the dough into the roll to seal well; stretch to make even.

With the sealed edge down, shape the roll into a ring on a lightly greased baking sheet. Pinch the ends together. With scissors, make cuts ⅔ of the way through ring at 1-inch intervals. Turn each section onto its side. Let rise until double, about 45 minutes.

Heat oven to 375°. Bake 25 to 30 minutes or until golden brown. While warm, frost the ring with Confectioners' Sugar Icing and decorate with nuts and candied cherry halves.

Three secrets for creating a Swedish Tea Ring as pretty perfect as this: **1.** Stretch and shape the ring evenly. **2.** Be sure the cuts are the same size all around. **3.** Carefully turn each section on its side.

BOHEMIAN BRAID

1 package active dry yeast
¼ cup warm water (105 to 115°)
¾ cup lukewarm milk (scalded then cooled)
¼ cup sugar
1 teaspoon salt
1 egg
¼ cup shortening
½ cup raisins
½ cup chopped blanched almonds
1 teaspoon grated lemon peel
⅛ teaspoon mace
3½ to 3¾ cups all-purpose flour*
1 egg yolk
2 tablespoons cold water
Confectioners' Sugar Icing (below)

*If using self-rising flour, omit salt.

Dissolve yeast in warm water. Stir in milk, sugar, salt, egg, shortening, raisins, almonds, lemon peel, mace and 1¾ cups of the flour. Beat until smooth. Mix in enough of the remaining flour to make the dough easy to handle.

Turn the dough onto a lightly floured board and knead until smooth and elastic, about 5 minutes. Place in a greased bowl; turn the greased side up. Cover and let rise in a warm place until double, about 1½ hours. (The dough is ready if an indentation remains when touched.)

Punch down the dough and let rise again until almost double, about 30 minutes.

Divide the dough into 4 equal parts; shape three of the parts into 14-inch strands. Place on a lightly greased baking sheet and braid loosely. Pinch ends together and fold under. Divide the remaining part into 3 pieces and shape each into a 12-inch strand. Braid these strands and place on the large braid. Cover and let rise until double, 45 to 60 minutes.

Heat oven to 350°. Mix egg yolk and cold water and brush on the braids. Bake 30 to 40 minutes or until golden brown. While warm, frost the braid with Confectioners' Sugar Icing and decorate with candied cherries and pecan halves.

CONFECTIONERS' SUGAR ICING

Mix 1 cup confectioners' sugar and about 1 tablespoon milk until smooth.

Braid strands loosely, being careful not to stretch the dough. Pinch ends together and fold under.

SOUR CREAM COFFEE CAKE

¾ cup soft butter
1½ cups sugar
3 eggs
1½ teaspoons vanilla
3 cups all-purpose flour*
1½ teaspoons baking powder
1½ teaspoons soda
¼ teaspoon salt
1½ cups dairy sour cream
Filling (below)

*If using self-rising flour, omit baking powder, soda and salt.

Heat oven to 350°. Grease a tube pan, 10×4 inches, a 12-cup bundt pan or 2 loaf pans, 9×5×3 inches. Combine butter, sugar, eggs and vanilla in a large mixer bowl. Beat on medium speed 2 minutes, scraping the bowl occasionally. (Or beat 300 strokes by hand.) Mix in flour, baking powder, soda and salt alternately with the sour cream.

For a tube or bundt pan, spread ⅓ of the batter (about 2 cups) in the pan and sprinkle with ⅓ of the Filling (about 6 tablespoons); repeat 2 times. For loaf pans, spread ¼ of the batter (about 1½ cups) in each pan and sprinkle with ¼ of the Filling (about 5 tablespoons); repeat.

Bake about 1 hour or until a wooden pick inserted in center comes out clean. Cool in pan(s) a few minutes.

FILLING

Mix ½ cup brown sugar (packed), ½ cup finely chopped nuts and 1½ teaspoons cinnamon.

BLUEBERRY BUCKLE COFFEE CAKE

2 cups all-purpose flour*
¾ cup sugar
2½ teaspoons baking powder
¾ teaspoon salt
¼ cup shortening
¾ cup milk
1 egg
2 cups fresh blueberries
Crumb Topping (below)

*If using self-rising flour, omit baking powder and salt.

Heat oven to 375°. Grease a baking pan, 9×9×2 inches, or a layer pan, 9×1½ inches. Blend flour, sugar, baking powder, salt, shortening, milk and egg; beat ½ minute. Carefully stir in blueberries.

Spread in the pan and sprinkle Crumb Topping on the batter. Bake 45 to 50 minutes or until a wooden pick inserted in center comes out clean. Serve warm.

CRUMB TOPPING

Mix ½ cup sugar, ⅓ cup all-purpose flour, ½ teaspoon cinnamon and ¼ cup soft butter.

FRENCH BREAKFAST PUFFS

⅓ cup shortening
½ cup sugar
1 egg
1½ cups all-purpose flour* or
cake flour
1½ teaspoons baking powder
½ teaspoon salt
¼ teaspoon nutmeg
½ cup milk
½ cup sugar
1 teaspoon cinnamon
½ cup butter or margarine, melted

*If using self-rising flour, omit baking powder and salt.

Heat oven to 350°. Grease 15 medium muffin cups (2¾ inches in diameter). Mix thoroughly shortening, ½ cup sugar and the egg. Stir in flour, baking powder, salt and nutmeg alternately with the milk. Fill the muffin cups ⅔ full. Bake 20 to 25 minutes.

Mix ½ cup sugar and the cinnamon. Immediately after baking, roll hot muffins in melted butter, then in the sugar-cinnamon mixture. Serve hot.

15 PUFFS.

TINY ALOHA PINEAPPLE MUFFINS

2 cups buttermilk baking mix
¼ cup sugar
2 tablespoons soft butter
1 egg
⅔ cup milk
½ cup well-drained crushed
pineapple
Thin Icing (below)
Chopped nuts

Heat oven to 400°. Grease 48 tiny muffin cups. Mix baking mix, sugar, butter, egg and milk with a fork and beat vigorously ½ minute. Fold in pineapple. Fill the muffin cups ⅔ full. Bake 12 to 15 minutes. While warm, frost with Thin Icing and sprinkle with nuts.

48 MUFFINS.

Note: The muffins can also be baked in 12 greased medium muffin cups. Bake 15 to 20 minutes.

THIN ICING

Mix ½ cup confectioners' sugar and 1 tablespoon water until smooth.

VARIATIONS

Banana Muffins: Omit the milk and pineapple and mix in 1 cup mashed very ripe banana.

Coconut Muffins: Omit the pineapple and fold in ½ cup flaked coconut.

DATE-NUT BREAD

1½ cups boiling water
1½ cups cut-up dates
½ cup brown sugar (packed)
1 tablespoon shortening
1 egg
2¼ cups all-purpose flour*
1 teaspoon soda
½ teaspoon salt
1 cup coarsely chopped nuts

*If using self-rising flour, decrease soda to ¼ teaspoon and omit salt.

Pour boiling water over the dates and cool.

Heat oven to 350°. Grease a loaf pan, 9 × 5 × 3 inches. Mix thoroughly brown sugar, shortening and egg. Stir in the date mixture. Mix in flour, soda and salt, then stir in nuts. Spread in the pan. Bake 60 to 70 minutes or until a wooden pick inserted in center comes out clean.

PUMPKIN BREAD

⅔ cup shortening
2⅔ cups sugar
4 eggs
1 can (16 ounces) pumpkin
⅔ cup water
3⅓ cups all-purpose flour*
2 teaspoons soda
1½ teaspoons salt
½ teaspoon baking powder
1 teaspoon cinnamon
1 teaspoon cloves
⅔ cup coarsely chopped nuts
⅔ cup raisins or cut-up dates

*If using self-rising flour, omit soda, salt and baking powder.

Heat oven to 350°. Grease 2 loaf pans, 9 × 5 × 3 inches, or 3 loaf pans, 8½ × 4½ × 2½ inches. Cream shortening and sugar thoroughly. Mix in eggs, pumpkin and water. Blend in flour, soda, salt, baking powder, cinnamon and cloves. Stir in nuts and raisins and spread in the pans. Bake 65 to 70 minutes or until a wooden pick inserted in center comes out clean.

2 LOAVES.

FLUFFY BUTTERMILK PANCAKES

3 egg yolks
1⅔ cups buttermilk*
1 teaspoon soda
1½ cups all-purpose flour**
1 teaspoon baking powder
½ teaspoon salt
1 tablespoon sugar
3 tablespoons soft butter or margarine
3 egg whites, stiffly beaten

*For thinner pancakes, increase the buttermilk to 1¾ cups.

**If using self-rising flour, decrease soda to ½ teaspoon and omit baking powder and salt.

Beat egg yolks with rotary beater. Add remaining ingredients except egg whites and beat until smooth. Gently fold in egg whites.

Grease heated griddle if necessary. (To test griddle, sprinkle with a few drops of water. If bubbles "skitter around," heat is just right.) Pour the batter onto the hot griddle from the tip of a large spoon or from a pitcher. Turn the pancakes as soon as they are puffed and full of bubbles but before the bubbles break. Bake other side until golden brown.

ABOUT SIXTEEN 4-INCH PANCAKES.

GOLDEN BUTTER WAFFLES

2 eggs
1¾ cups milk
½ cup butter or margarine, melted
2 cups all-purpose flour*
4 teaspoons baking powder
½ teaspoon salt
1 tablespoon sugar

*If using self-rising flour, omit baking powder and salt.

Heat waffle iron. Beat eggs until fluffy with rotary beater. Add the remaining ingredients and beat until smooth.

Pour the batter from a cup or pitcher onto the center of the hot waffle iron. Bake until steaming stops, about 5 minutes. Remove waffle carefully.

THREE 10-INCH WAFFLES.

TOPPINGS

Honey Butter: Beat ½ cup honey, ½ cup soft butter and 1 teaspoon grated orange peel until fluffy.

Maple-Apricot Syrup: Heat ¾ cup maple-flavored syrup, 1 tablespoon butter and ¼ cup apricot nectar to boiling, stirring occasionally. Serve warm.

Maple Rum-flavored Syrup: Heat 1 cup maple-flavored syrup and 1 tablespoon butter to boiling. Remove from heat and stir in ½ teaspoon rum flavoring. Serve warm.

WHIPPED CREAM DOUGHNUTS

1 package active dry yeast
¼ cup warm water (105 to 115°)
2 eggs
1 cup whipping cream
1 teaspoon vanilla
⅓ cup sugar
3½ cups all-purpose flour*
1 tablespoon baking powder
1 teaspoon salt
¼ teaspoon cinnamon
¼ teaspoon nutmeg

*If using self-rising flour, omit baking powder and salt.

Dissolve yeast in warm water. In a small mixer bowl, beat eggs, whipping cream, vanilla and sugar until light and fluffy. Stir into yeast. Mix in the remaining ingredients until the dough is soft and easy to handle.

In a deep fat fryer or kettle, heat fat or oil (3 to 4 inches deep) to 375°. (The fat is hot enough if a 1-inch cube of bread browns in 60 seconds.) Roll the dough about ⅓ inch thick on a lightly floured cloth-covered board and cut with a floured doughnut cutter.

Drop doughnuts into the hot fat and turn as they rise to the surface. Fry until golden brown on both sides, about 2 minutes. Avoid pricking the doughnuts when removing them from the fat. Drain on paper towels. Serve plain, sugared or frosted.

2 DOZEN DOUGHNUTS.

Note: Fry the doughnut "holes" as a special treat for the children.

VARIATIONS

Bear Tracks: Roll the dough ⅓ inch thick on a lightly floured cloth-covered board and cut into strips, 3 × 1 inch. With a sharp knife, make cuts ½ inch apart and halfway through on one side of each strip. Fry as for doughnuts.

Turnabouts: Turn half the dough onto a lightly floured cloth-covered board. Roll into a rectangle, 15 × 5 inches, and cut into twelve 2½-inch squares. Cut a diagonal slit in each square. Draw a corner through the slit and curl back in the opposite direction. Repeat with the other half of the dough. Fry as for doughnuts.

Raised doughnut versus cake doughnut. Which is the best? No need to choose. Our recipe combines the best of the two doughnut worlds. What's more, you can change the shape of this doughnut; cut the rolled dough into a variety of shapes—hearts for Valentine's Day, stars for Christmas.

But what of the doughnut's famous hole? Some give credit to a 19th-century Maine sea captain who had had his fill of his mother's soggy-centered fried cakes and testily instructed her to "cut a hole in the middle where it doesn't cook." Others say it all happened much earlier. They tell of a Nauset Indian who playfully shot an arrow right through one of his wife's fried cakes. As she scurried away in fright, she dropped the perforated patty into a kettle of boiling grease. Today, the "missing" hole is as delicious as the ring.

Cakes

Cakes

A cake can speak for you in many ways. It tells your family you love them. Or bids a warm welcome to your friends. It wishes a jolly birthday. Or says thank-you for a favor. And for saying what comes naturally graciously, there's nothing quite like those tried-and-true cakes that have earned the title of All-Time Favorites.

Take one of the oldest of these recipes, the Bonnie Butter Cake. It's still saying "Hi, neighbor." with happy hospitality. And the elegant Lemon-filled Coconut, an example of survival of the prettiest, continues to shine as the grand finale for Sunday dinner with the relatives. Best Chocolate Cake, descendant of the little square Brown Beauty, carries on the tradition of cheering up a rainy day. Another nice thing about these ageless beauties is that they've willingly adapted to modern ways. With today's ingredients and today's equipment, they pull themselves together in minutes. Which makes saying it with a cake a pleasure for the one who mans the mixer, too.

There are other sweet talkers here, too—relative newcomers on the scene. You'll re-meet the "first really new cake in a hundred years," born in 1948. It's the light and airy Chiffon, of course, a cake of many party moods. For saying congratulations to someone you care about, try a masterful cake mix creation. There's Triple Fudge, for those who like their chocolate big, and the magnificent Velvet Cream, a multilayer tribute.

From homespun to glamorous, from scratch recipe to mix, here are the cakes you've praised the most over the years. And they all say love and affection in the most delicious way.

On the preceding pages:
Bonnie Butter Cake,
Williamsburg Orange Cake,
Lemon Velvet Cream Cake,
Lemon-filled Coconut Cake,
Daffodil Cake

LEMON-FILLED COCONUT CAKE

2¼ cups cake flour or
    2 cups all-purpose flour*
1½ cups sugar
3½ teaspoons baking powder
 1 teaspoon salt
½ cup shortening
 1 cup milk
 1 teaspoon vanilla
 4 egg whites (½ cup)
    Clear Lemon Filling (below)
    White Mountain Frosting
    (page 102)
 1 cup flaked or shredded coconut

*Do not use self-rising flour in this recipe.

No wonder this basic white cake is also called Silver White—its "sterling" qualities of lightness and richness can't be beat. So reliable that you can mix and match it with almost any assortment of frostings and fillings. Here are just a few ideas: Williamsburg Butter Frosting, inside and out; Butterscotch Filling with a Marshmallow Frosting; Fudge or Penuche Frosting. Let your imagination take it from here.

Heat oven to 350°. Grease and flour a baking pan, 13 × 9 × 2 inches, or 2 layer pans, 8 or 9 × 1½ inches. Measure flour, sugar, baking powder, salt, shortening, milk and vanilla into a large mixer bowl. Blend ½ minute on low speed, scraping the bowl constantly. Beat 2 minutes on high speed, scraping occasionally. Add egg whites and beat 2 minutes on high speed, scraping the bowl occasionally. Pour into the pan(s).

Bake the oblong 35 to 40 minutes, the layers 30 to 35 minutes or until a wooden pick inserted in center comes out clean. Cool.

Spread the oblong cake or fill the layer cake with Clear Lemon Filling and frost with White Mountain Frosting. (With the oblong cake, the frosting goes right on the filling.) Sprinkle with coconut.

CLEAR LEMON FILLING

¾ cup sugar
3 tablespoons cornstarch
¼ teaspoon salt
¾ cup water
1 teaspoon grated lemon peel
1 tablespoon butter or margarine
⅓ cup lemon juice
4 drops yellow food color, if desired

Mix sugar, cornstarch and salt in a saucepan. Gradually stir in the water. Cook, stirring constantly, until the mixture thickens and boils. Boil and stir 1 minute.

Remove from heat and add lemon peel and butter. Gradually stir in lemon juice and food color. Cool thoroughly. If the filling is too soft, refrigerate until set.

BONNIE BUTTER CAKE

⅔ cup butter or margarine, softened
1¾ cups granulated sugar
2 eggs (⅓ to ½ cup)
1½ teaspoons vanilla
3 cups cake flour or 2¾ cups all-purpose flour*
2½ teaspoons baking powder
1 teaspoon salt
1¼ cups milk
Egyptian Filling (below)
1 cup chilled whipping cream
2 tablespoons confectioners' sugar

*If using self-rising flour, omit baking powder and salt.

Take special note of this rich and unusual filling—we've had raves on it year after year. Some home-testers tell us it's best with a white layer cake; others prefer it as a topping for devils food squares. Still others use it as a filling *and* on top, as we did here with one of our butteriest yellow cakes. How do you cast your ballot?

Heat oven to 350°. Grease and flour 2 layer pans, 9 × 1½ inches. In a large mixer bowl, mix the butter, granulated sugar, eggs and vanilla until fluffy. Beat 5 minutes on high speed, scraping the bowl occasionally. On low speed, mix in flour, baking powder and salt alternately with the milk. Pour into the pans.

Bake 30 to 35 minutes or until a wooden pick inserted in center comes out clean. Cool.

Spread Egyptian Filling between the layers and on top of the cake. In a chilled bowl, beat the whipping cream and confectioners' sugar until stiff; spread on side of cake. Refrigerate cake until serving time.

EGYPTIAN FILLING

⅔ cup light cream (20%)
⅔ cup sugar
2 egg yolks, slightly beaten
½ cup cut-up dates
½ teaspoon vanilla
½ cup chopped toasted almonds

Mix light cream, sugar, egg yolks and dates in a small saucepan. Cook over low heat, stirring constantly, until slightly thickened—5 to 6 minutes. Remove from heat and stir in vanilla and nuts. Cool.

BEST CHOCOLATE CAKE

2 cups all-purpose flour* or
   cake flour
2 cups sugar
1 teaspoon soda
1 teaspoon salt
½ teaspoon baking powder
¾ cup water
¾ cup buttermilk
½ cup shortening
2 eggs (⅓ to ½ cup)
1 teaspoon vanilla
4 ounces melted unsweetened
   chocolate (cool)
   Satiny Beige Frosting (page 102)
   or Fudge Frosting (page 103)

*If using self-rising flour, omit salt and baking powder.

Heat oven to 350°. Grease and flour a baking pan, 13×9×2 inches, or two 9-inch or three 8-inch round layer pans.

Measure all ingredients except the frosting into a large mixer bowl. Blend ½ minute on low speed, scraping the bowl constantly. Beat 3 minutes on high speed, scraping occasionally. Pour into the pan(s).

Bake oblong 40 to 45 minutes, layers 30 to 35 minutes or until a wooden pick inserted in center comes out clean. Cool; frost cake with Satiny Beige Frosting.

BROWNIE NUT CAKE

1¼ cups all-purpose flour* or
   cake flour
1⅓ cups sugar
1¼ teaspoons baking powder
½ teaspoon salt
¼ teaspoon soda
1 cup milk
3 tablespoons shortening
1 egg
½ teaspoon vanilla
3 ounces melted unsweetened
   chocolate (cool)
⅔ cup chopped nuts
   Quick Fudge Frosting (page 103)

*If using self-rising flour, omit baking powder and salt.

Heat oven to 350°. Grease and flour a baking pan, 8×8×2 or 9×9×2 inches. Measure all ingredients except the frosting into a large mixer bowl. Blend ½ minute on low speed, scraping the bowl constantly. Beat 3 minutes on high speed, scraping occasionally. Pour into the pan.

Bake 40 to 50 minutes or until a wooden pick inserted in center comes out clean. Cool; frost cake with Quick Fudge Frosting.

CHOCOLATE BUTTERMALLOW CAKE

1¾ cups all-purpose flour* or
  cake flour
1 cup granulated sugar
½ cup brown sugar (packed)
1½ teaspoons soda
¾ teaspoon salt
1¼ cups buttermilk
½ cup shortening
2 eggs (⅓ to ½ cup)
2 ounces melted unsweetened
  chocolate (cool)
1 teaspoon vanilla
½ teaspoon red food color
  Butterscotch Filling (below)
½ cup finely chopped nuts
  Marshmallow Frosting (below)

*Do not use self-rising flour in this recipe.

Our special treatment of Red Devils
Food Cake calls for two tempting
toppings, one right on top of
the other. The result: a new family
favorite.

If you don't have an oblong tray,
you can improvise (and prettily,
too) by covering a piece of card-
board with a colorful foil wrapping
paper. Or, if you prefer, leave the
cake right in the pan and frost only
the top. Admittedly, it's easier
that way. And if your house is full
of cake snackers, it's probably
more practical, too.

Heat oven to 350°. Grease and flour a baking pan, 13 × 9 × 2 inches. Measure all ingredients except the filling, nuts and frosting into a large mixer bowl. Blend ½ minute on low speed, scraping the bowl constantly. Beat 3 minutes on high speed, scraping occasionally. Pour into the pan. Bake 40 minutes or until a wooden pick inserted in center comes out clean. Cool 10 minutes, then remove the cake from the pan and cool completely.

Spread Butterscotch Filling on top of cake to within ½ inch of edge; sprinkle with nuts. Frost sides and top with Marshmallow Frosting. If desired, drizzle melted chocolate on the frosting.

BUTTERSCOTCH FILLING

Mix 1 cup brown sugar (packed) and 3 tablespoons flour in a saucepan. Gradually stir in ¾ cup light cream. Heat to boiling, stirring constantly. Boil and stir 1 minute. Remove from heat and blend in 2 tablespoons butter or margarine and 1 teaspoon vanilla. Cool.

MARSHMALLOW FROSTING

2 egg whites
1½ cups sugar
¼ teaspoon cream of tartar
1 tablespoon light corn syrup
⅓ cup water
1½ cups miniature marshmallows

Combine egg whites, sugar, cream of tartar, syrup and water in the top of a double boiler. Blend on low speed with an electric mixer 1 minute. Place over boiling water and beat on high speed until stiff peaks form, about 7 minutes. Remove from heat and add marshmallows. Continue beating until the frosting is of spreading consistency.

VELVET CREAM CAKE

1 package (14.3 or 15.4 ounces) creamy-type frosting mix
1½ cups whipping cream
1 teaspoon vanilla
1 package (18.5 ounces) layer cake mix
Thin Icing (below)
Chopped nuts

Here's a nomination for *the* perfect party cake. The four torte-thin layers take to all sorts of elegant garnishings, with fruit, nuts, little candies, even marzipan. It's got mix-quick timing and, perhaps best of all, is guaranteed to serve at least 12 people.

What's more, there's almost no limit to the mixing and matching possibilities of this chameleon-like cake. (And that's precisely why we developed it—to give you a way to add your own personal touch to convenient cake mixes.) We've suggested a few of our favorite combinations here—but you can create your own custom blends, too.

Combine 2 cups of the frosting mix (dry), the whipping cream and vanilla in a small mixer bowl. Cover and chill 1 hour. Reserve the remaining frosting mix.

Bake the cake in 2 layer pans, 9 × 1½ inches, as directed on the package. Cool. Split layers horizontally to make 4 layers.

Blend the chilled frosting mix and whipping cream and beat on medium speed until stiff; fill the layers. Frost the top of the cake with Thin Icing, allowing some to drizzle down the side. Sprinkle with chopped nuts. Refrigerate until ready to serve.

THIN ICING

Beat reserved frosting mix, 2 to 3 tablespoons hot water and 1 tablespoon light corn syrup until smooth. If necessary, stir in 1 to 2 teaspoons water until the mixture is of glaze consistency.

VARIATIONS

Chocolate Mocha Cream Cake: Use chocolate fudge frosting mix and devils food cake mix. Add 1 teaspoon powdered instant coffee to the frosting mix-whipping cream mixture. Garnish cake with diced roasted almonds.

Lemon Cream Cake: Use creamy lemon frosting mix and lemon cake mix. Sprinkle cake with pistachio nuts.

Strawberry Cream Cake: Use creamy white frosting mix and white cake mix. Add 1 tablespoon lemon juice to the frosting mix-whipping cream mixture. After beating the mixture, fold in 1 cup crushed fresh strawberries, well drained (about 1 quart). Garnish cake with whole strawberries.

2¼ cups cake flour or 2 cups
all-purpose flour*
1½ cups sugar
3 teaspoons baking powder
1 teaspoon salt
½ cup salad oil
5 egg yolks (with cake flour) or
7 egg yolks (with all-purpose
flour)
¾ cup cold water
2 tablespoons grated orange
peel
1 cup egg whites (7 or 8)
½ teaspoon cream of tartar
Orange Glaze (below)

*If using self-rising flour, omit baking powder and
salt.

To fold the egg yolk mixture into the
beaten whites, carefully cut down
through the center of the whites,
along the bottom and up the side.

ORANGE CHIFFON CAKE

Heat oven to 325°. Stir together flour, sugar, baking powder and salt in a medium mixing bowl. Make a well and add *in order:* oil, egg yolks, water and orange peel. Beat with a spoon until smooth; set aside.

Measure the egg whites and cream of tartar into a large mixer bowl. Beat until whites form very stiff peaks. *Do not underbeat.* (As a test, draw a rubber scraper through the beaten whites; it should leave a clear path.) Gradually pour the egg yolk mixture over the beaten whites, gently folding *just* until blended. (Pour about ½ cup of the egg yolk mixture at a time over beaten egg whites. To fold, use a rubber scraper to cut down through the center of whites, along bottom of bowl and up the side, giving the bowl a quarter-turn each time. Repeat.) Do not overfold or the mixture will lose air. Pour into an ungreased tube pan, 10 × 4 inches.

Bake on lowest rack 1 hour 15 minutes or until the top springs back when touched lightly with a finger. Immediately invert the tube pan on a funnel; let hang until the cake is completely cool, at least 2 hours.

Remove cake from pan. Pour or spoon Orange Glaze over top of cake and spread, allowing some to drizzle unevenly down side of cake.

ORANGE GLAZE

⅓ cup butter or margarine
2 cups confectioners' sugar
½ teaspoon grated orange peel
2 to 4 tablespoons orange juice

Melt butter in a saucepan. Mix in sugar and orange peel. Stir in orange juice, 1 tablespoon at a time, until the mixture is of glaze consistency.

DAFFODIL CAKE

1 cup cake flour
¾ cup plus 2 tablespoons sugar
12 egg whites (1½ cups)
1½ teaspoons cream of tartar
¼ teaspoon salt
¾ cup sugar
6 egg yolks
1½ teaspoons vanilla
½ teaspoon almond extract
Lemon Glaze (below)

Heat oven to 375°. Blend flour and ¾ cup plus 2 tablespoons sugar and set aside.

Measure egg whites, cream of tartar and salt into a large mixer bowl. Beat on medium speed until foamy. Add ¾ cup sugar, 2 tablespoons at a time, beating on high speed until the meringue holds stiff, glossy peaks.

In a small mixer bowl, beat egg yolks until very thick and lemon colored, about 5 minutes.

Fold flavorings into the meringue. Then sprinkle the flour-sugar mixture, ¼ at a time, over the meringue, folding in carefully just until the flour-sugar mixture disappears. Pour half the batter into another bowl; gently fold in egg yolks.

Spoon the yellow and white batters alternately into an ungreased tube pan, 10×4 inches. Gently cut through the batters to make a swirling effect.

Bake on the lowest rack of the oven about 40 minutes or until top springs back when touched lightly with finger.

Immediately invert the tube pan on a funnel and let hang until the cake is completely cool, at least 2 hours. Spread the cake with Lemon Glaze.

LEMON GLAZE

1 cup confectioners' sugar
½ teaspoon grated lemon peel
1 teaspoon lemon juice
About 2 tablespoons milk
1 drop yellow food color

Mix all ingredients until smooth.

ANGEL FOOD DELUXE

1 cup cake flour
1½ cups confectioners' sugar
12 egg whites (1½ cups)
1½ teaspoons cream of tartar
¼ teaspoon salt
1 cup granulated sugar
1½ teaspoons vanilla
½ teaspoon almond extract

Heat oven to 375°. Blend flour and confectioners' sugar and set aside. (For easy blending, sift the flour and confectioners' sugar together.) Measure egg whites, cream of tartar and salt into a large mixer bowl. Beat on medium speed until foamy. Add granulated sugar, 2 tablespoons at a time, beating on high speed until the meringue holds stiff, glossy peaks.

Gently fold in flavorings. Sprinkle the flour-sugar mixture, ¼ cup at a time, over meringue, folding in gently just until the flour-sugar mixture disappears. Carefully push the batter into an ungreased tube pan, 10 × 4 inches. Gently cut through batter with a rubber scraper to break air holes.

Bake on lowest rack 30 to 35 minutes or until a deep golden brown and the top springs back when touched lightly with finger. Immediately invert the tube pan on a funnel and let hang until the cake is completely cool, at least 2 hours.

ANGEL ALEXANDER

Angel Food Deluxe (above)
2 tablespoons light cream (20%)
½ cup dark crème de cacao
1½ cups chilled whipping cream
¼ cup confectioners' sugar

Bake the cake as directed. Cool in the pan.

Several hours before serving, combine cream and crème de cacao. With a 5-inch wooden skewer, make many holes of varying depths in the cake. Pour half the crème de cacao mixture into the holes; let cake stand in pan 2 hours.

Invert cake onto serving plate. Make more holes in top and pour in remaining crème de cacao.

In a chilled bowl, beat whipping cream and sugar just until stiff; frost side and top of cake. Refrigerate cake until serving time.

ANGEL FOOD WALDORF

Angel Food Deluxe
(page 96)
- 3 cups whipping cream
- 1½ cups confectioners' sugar
- ¾ cup cocoa
- ¼ teaspoon salt
- ⅔ cup toasted slivered blanched almonds

Bake the cake as directed; cool. Meanwhile, combine whipping cream, confectioners' sugar, cocoa and salt in a mixer bowl. Cover and chill at least 1 hour.

Remove the cake from the pan and place upside down. Slice off the entire top of cake about 1 inch down and set aside. Make cuts down into cake 1 inch from outer edge and 1 inch from the edge of hole, leaving substantial "walls" on each side. With a curved knife or a spoon, scoop out the cake within the cuts, being careful to leave a base of cake 1 inch thick. Place cake on a serving plate.

Beat the chilled cocoa mixture until stiff. Fold ⅓ cup almonds into half the cocoa mixture. Spoon the mixture into the cake cavity, pressing in firmly to avoid holes in cut slices. Replace the top of cake. Frost with remaining cocoa mixture; sprinkle with remaining almonds. Chill at least 4 hours.

12 TO 16 SERVINGS.

Be sure to fill every little space between the "walls" of the cake—don't be afraid to press the cocoa mixture in firmly. And for perfect slices, like the one at right, wipe the knife with a damp towel after making each cut.

A cake roll in the old-time tradition . . . awhirl with a sparkling jelly and sprinkled with confectioners' sugar.

1. In order to roll the cake easily, it must be hot. And don't forget the towel—it keeps the cake from sticking together.

2. Unroll the cooled cake carefully so it doesn't crack; immediately spread it with jelly and reroll.

OLD-FASHIONED JELLY ROLL

3 eggs (½ to ⅔ cup)
1 cup granulated sugar
⅓ cup water
1 teaspoon vanilla
1 cup cake flour or ¾ cup
  all-purpose flour*
1 teaspoon baking powder
¼ teaspoon salt
  About ⅔ cup jelly or jam
  Confectioners' sugar

*If using self-rising flour, omit baking powder and salt.

Heat oven to 375°. Line a jelly roll pan, 15½ × 10½ × 1 inch, with aluminum foil or waxed paper, then grease. In a small mixer bowl, beat eggs until very thick and lemon colored, about 5 minutes. Pour eggs into a large mixer bowl and gradually beat in granulated sugar. On low speed, blend in water and vanilla. Gradually add flour, baking powder and salt, beating just until the batter is smooth. Pour into the pan, spreading the batter into the corners.

Bake 12 to 15 minutes or until a wooden pick inserted in center comes out clean. Loosen cake from the edges of the pan immediately and invert on a towel that's generously sprinkled with confectioners' sugar. Carefully remove the foil. Trim off the cake's edges if they're very crisp so that it will not split when rolled.

While hot, carefully roll cake *and towel* from narrow end. Cool on a wire rack at least 30 minutes. Unroll cake and remove towel. Beat jelly with fork just enough to soften; spread over cake. Roll up and sprinkle with confectioners' sugar.

10 SERVINGS.

VARIATIONS

Cream Roll: Omit the jelly. In a chilled bowl, beat 1 cup chilled whipping cream and 2 tablespoons confectioners' sugar until stiff. Spread on unrolled cake. Serve roll with sweetened sliced fresh strawberries or peaches.

Ice-cream or Sherbet Roll: Omit the jelly. Slightly soften 1 pint of your favorite ice cream or sherbet and spread on unrolled cake. Freeze roll several hours or until firm.

DATE CAKE

1⅔ cups all-purpose flour*
1 cup sugar
1 teaspoon soda
½ teaspoon salt
1 cup water
¼ cup shortening
1 egg
1 teaspoon vanilla
1 cup cut-up dates**
½ cup finely chopped nuts
    Chocolate Chip-Nut Topping
    (right)

*If using self-rising flour, decrease soda to ¼ teaspoon, omit salt and use 2 eggs.

**Packaged chopped dates (sugar coated) can be substituted for the cut-up dates.

Heat oven to 350°. Grease and flour a baking pan, 9×9×2 inches. Measure all ingredients except the topping into a large mixer bowl. Blend ½ minute on low speed, scraping the bowl constantly. Beat 3 minutes on high speed, scraping occasionally. Pour into the pan and sprinkle Chocolate Chip-Nut Topping on batter. Bake 45 to 50 minutes or until a wooden pick inserted in center comes out clean.

CHOCOLATE CHIP-NUT TOPPING

Mix ½ cup semisweet chocolate pieces, 2 tablespoons sugar and ½ cup finely chopped nuts.

JEWELED FRUITCAKE

1 package (8 ounces) dried
    apricots (about 2 cups)
1 package (8 ounces) pitted
    dates (1½ cups)
¾ pound whole Brazil nuts
    (1½ cups)
1 cup drained red and green
    maraschino cherries
⅓ pound red and green
    candied pineapple, cut up
    (about 1 cup)
¾ cup all-purpose flour*
¾ cup sugar
½ teaspoon baking powder
½ teaspoon salt
3 eggs (½ to ⅔ cup)
1½ teaspoons vanilla

*If using self-rising flour, omit baking powder and salt.

Heat oven to 300°. Line a loaf pan, 9×5×3 or 8½×4½×2½ inches, with aluminum foil, then grease the foil. Leaving the apricots, dates, nuts and cherries whole, mix all ingredients thoroughly. Spread the mixture evenly in the pan.

Bake 1 hour 45 minutes or until a wooden pick inserted in center comes out clean. If necessary, cover with aluminum foil for the last 30 minutes of baking to prevent excessive browning. Remove from pan and cool. Wrap the fruitcake in plastic wrap or aluminum foil and store in a cool place.

WILLIAMSBURG ORANGE CAKE

2¾ cups cake flour or 2½ cups all-purpose flour*
1½ cups sugar
1½ teaspoons soda
¾ teaspoon salt
1½ cups buttermilk
½ cup butter or margarine, softened
¼ cup shortening
3 eggs (½ to ⅔ cup)
1½ teaspoons vanilla
1 cup golden raisins, cut up
½ cup finely chopped nuts
1 tablespoon grated orange peel
Williamsburg Butter Frosting (right)

*Do not use self-rising flour in this recipe.

Heat oven to 350°. Grease and flour 3 layer pans, 8 × 1½ inches. Measure all ingredients except the frosting into a large mixer bowl. Blend ½ minute on low speed, scraping the bowl constantly. Beat 3 minutes on high speed, scraping occasionally. Pour into the pans.

Bake 30 to 35 minutes or until a wooden pick inserted in center comes out clean. Cool; fill and frost cake with Williamsburg Butter Frosting.

WILLIAMSBURG BUTTER FROSTING

½ cup soft butter or margarine
4½ cups confectioners' sugar
4 to 5 tablespoons orange-flavored liqueur or orange juice
1 tablespoon grated orange peel

Blend butter and sugar. Stir in liqueur and orange peel and beat until smooth.

APPLESAUCE CAKE

2½ cups all-purpose flour* or cake flour
2 cups sugar
1½ teaspoons soda
1½ teaspoons salt
¼ teaspoon baking powder
¾ teaspoon cinnamon
½ teaspoon cloves
½ teaspoon allspice
1½ cups canned applesauce
½ cup water
½ cup shortening
2 eggs (⅓ to ½ cup)
1 cup raisins
½ cup finely chopped walnuts
Penuche Frosting (page 102)

*Do not use self-rising flour in this recipe.

Heat oven to 350°. Grease and flour a baking pan, 13 × 9 × 2 inches, or 2 layer pans, 8 or 9 × 1½ inches. Measure all ingredients except the frosting into a large mixer bowl. Blend ½ minute on low speed, scraping the bowl constantly. Beat 3 minutes on high speed, scraping occasionally. Pour into the pan(s).

Bake oblong 60 to 65 minutes, layers 50 to 55 minutes or until a wooden pick inserted in center comes out clean. Cool; frost cake with Penuche Frosting.

WHITE MOUNTAIN FROSTING

½ cup sugar
¼ cup light corn syrup
2 tablespoons water
2 egg whites (¼ cup)
1 teaspoon vanilla

Combine sugar, corn syrup and water in a small saucepan. Cover and heat to a rolling boil over medium heat. Uncover and boil rapidly, without stirring, to 242° on a candy thermometer or until a small amount of the mixture forms a firm ball when dropped into very cold water.

As the mixture boils, beat egg whites in a small mixer bowl until stiff peaks form. Pour the hot syrup very slowly and in a thin stream into the beaten egg whites, beating constantly on medium speed. Beat on high speed until stiff peaks form. Add vanilla during the last minute of beating.

FROSTS A 13×9-INCH CAKE OR FILLS AND FROSTS TWO 8- OR 9-INCH LAYERS.

VARIATION

Satiny Beige Frosting: Substitute ½ cup brown sugar (packed) for the granulated sugar and decrease the vanilla to ½ teaspoon.

PENUCHE FROSTING

½ cup butter or margarine
1 cup brown sugar (packed)
¼ cup milk
2 cups confectioners' sugar

Melt butter in a medium saucepan and stir in brown sugar. Heat to boiling, stirring constantly. Boil and stir over low heat 2 minutes. Stir in milk and heat to boiling. Remove from heat and cool to lukewarm.

Gradually stir in confectioners' sugar. Place the pan in a bowl of ice and water. Beat the frosting until smooth and of spreading consistency.

FROSTS A 13×9-INCH CAKE OR FILLS AND FROSTS TWO 8- OR 9-INCH LAYERS.

FUDGE FROSTING

2 cups sugar
¼ cup light corn syrup
½ cup milk
½ cup shortening
2 ounces unsweetened chocolate
¼ teaspoon salt
1 teaspoon vanilla

Combine all ingredients except the vanilla in medium saucepan. Cook over medium heat, stirring constantly, until chocolate is melted and sugar is dissolved. Heat to rolling boil, stirring constantly. Boil rapidly, stirring constantly, 1 minute or to 220° on a candy thermometer. Remove from heat and stir in vanilla.

Place the pan in a bowl of ice and water to cool slightly, about 5 minutes. Beat the frosting until it loses its gloss and is of spreading consistency, about 10 minutes.

FROSTS A 13×9-INCH CAKE OR FILLS AND FROSTS TWO 8- OR 9-INCH LAYERS.

QUICK FUDGE FROSTING

½ cup granulated sugar
2 tablespoons cocoa
2 tablespoons butter or margarine
¼ cup milk
1 tablespoon light corn syrup
Dash of salt
½ to ¾ cup confectioners' sugar
½ teaspoon vanilla

Mix granulated sugar and cocoa in a saucepan. Add butter, milk, corn syrup and salt and heat to boiling, stirring frequently. Boil vigorously 3 minutes, stirring occasionally. Cool. Beat in confectioners' sugar and vanilla.

FROSTS AN 8- OR 9-INCH SQUARE CAKE.

BROWNED BUTTER ICING

⅓ cup soft butter or margarine
3 cups confectioners' sugar
1½ teaspoons vanilla
About 2 tablespoons milk

Heat butter in a saucepan over medium heat just until a delicate brown. Blend in sugar. Stir in vanilla and milk and beat until the icing is smooth and of spreading consistency.

FROSTS A 13×9-INCH CAKE OR FILLS AND FROSTS TWO 8- OR 9-INCH LAYERS.

Cookies

Cookies

Look a cookie straight in the face and it's almost impossible to keep from smiling. Cookies are the happiness foods—dispensers of joy wherever they go, whatever the occasion. And we have scads of smile-proof cookies, collected over the years.

For homey cookies, you'll find some popular touches of Americana. Good old Peanut Butter Cookies, rich and peanutty and flattened with a fork. Snickerdoodles, with their coating of cinnamon and sugar. Big, fat Jumbo Molasses Cookies that fill the kitchen with the heavenly scents of spices and molasses. All three are good travelers, too. If wrapped separately and layered carefully, they can circle the globe with goodwill.

At holiday time, sample some of our inventive Christmas creations. Colorful Marzipan Cookies, inspired by the decorative fruit-shaped candies of Central Europe, practically shout of good cheer. And Candy Canes, one of the most asked-for cookies in the entire collection, can trim the tree as well as the table.

For year-round party sweets, there are traditional tea-tray favorites—but with those personal touches you tell us you like. Brownie Confections, for example, start with the classic brownie but add two toppings: a fondant-like frosting under melted chocolate. Dainty double-deck Cream Wafers resemble layers of sweet, flaky pastry, but with candy-colored fillings. And our very special Deluxe Sugar Cookies are extra thin and extra rich.

Other familiar cookie faces are here, too. See which one makes you smile the most. Then bake up a batch—and pass a little of that happiness around.

On the preceding pages:
TOP: Deluxe Sugar Cookies, Brownies, Salted Peanut Crisps
BOTTOM: Date-Nut Squares, Old-fashioned Oatmeal Cookies, Russian Teacakes

BROWNIES

4 ounces unsweetened
  chocolate
⅔ cup shortening
2 cups sugar
4 eggs
1 teaspoon vanilla
1¼ cups all-purpose flour*
1 teaspoon baking powder
1 teaspoon salt
1 cup chopped nuts

*If using self-rising flour, omit baking powder and salt.

Heat oven to 350°. Grease a baking pan, 13×9×2 inches. Melt chocolate and shortening in a large saucepan over low heat. Remove from heat and mix in the sugar, eggs and vanilla. Stir in the remaining ingredients. Spread in the pan.

Bake 30 minutes or until the brownies start to pull away from the sides of the pan. Do not overbake. Cool slightly. Cut into bars, about 2×1½ inches. For a change, spread brownies with Fudge Frosting (page 103) or dust with confectioners' sugar before cutting.

32 BARS.

VARIATION

Peanut Butter Brownies: Decrease shortening to ¼ cup and omit the nuts. Stir in ¼ cup peanut butter and ½ cup chopped peanuts.

BROWNIE CONFECTIONS

Brownies (above) or
1 package (22.5 ounces)
  fudge brownie mix
¼ cup butter
2 cups confectioners' sugar
2 tablespoons light cream
1 teaspoon vanilla
1 square (1 ounce)
  unsweetened chocolate
1 tablespoon butter

Bake Brownies as directed. Cool.

Heat ¼ cup butter over medium heat until it becomes a delicate brown. Blend in confectioners' sugar. Beat in light cream and vanilla until the frosting is smooth and of spreading consistency. Frost the brownies.

Melt chocolate and 1 tablespoon butter. Cool; spread a thin coating over the frosting. When both toppings are set, cut brownies into 1½-inch squares.

48 SQUARES.

COCONUT-CHOCOLATE MERINGUE BARS

¾ cup butter or margarine, softened
½ cup brown sugar (packed)
½ cup granulated sugar
3 eggs, separated
1 teaspoon vanilla
2 cups all-purpose flour*
1 teaspoon baking powder
¼ teaspoon soda
¼ teaspoon salt
1 package (6 ounces) semisweet chocolate pieces
1 cup flaked or grated coconut
¾ cup coarsely chopped nuts
1 cup brown sugar (packed)

*If using self-rising flour, omit baking powder, soda and salt.

Heat oven to 350°. Grease a baking pan, 13 × 9 × 2 inches. Blend butter, ½ cup brown sugar, the granulated sugar, egg yolks and vanilla. Beat about 2 minutes on medium speed with a mixer, scraping the bowl constantly, or by hand until smooth and well blended. Stir in flour, baking powder, soda and salt. Spread the dough in the pan and sprinkle with chocolate pieces, coconut and nuts.

Beat egg whites until foamy. Beat in 1 cup brown sugar, 1 tablespoon at a time, and continue beating until stiff and glossy—about 3 minutes. Spread on the chocolate-coconut-nut mixture. Bake 35 to 40 minutes. Cool; cut into bars, about 3 × 1 inch.

32 BARS.

LEMON-COCONUT SQUARES

1 cup all-purpose flour*
½ cup butter or margarine, softened
¼ cup confectioners' sugar
2 eggs
1 cup granulated sugar
½ teaspoon baking powder
¼ teaspoon salt
2 teaspoons lemon peel, if desired
2 tablespoons lemon juice
½ cup flaked coconut

*If using self-rising flour, omit baking powder and salt.

Heat oven to 350°. Mix thoroughly flour, butter and confectioners' sugar. Press evenly in an ungreased baking pan, 8 × 8 × 2 inches, building up a ½-inch edge. Bake 20 minutes.

Beat remaining ingredients except the coconut until light and fluffy, about 3 minutes. Stir in coconut and spread the mixture on the hot crust. Bake about 25 minutes longer, just until no impression remains when touched lightly in the center. Cool and cut into squares.

25 SQUARES.

Note: If you like, the coconut can be omitted.

DATE-NUT SQUARES

2 eggs
½ cup sugar
½ teaspoon vanilla
½ cup all-purpose flour*
½ teaspoon baking powder
½ teaspoon salt
2 cups cut-up dates
1 cup chopped nuts

*If using self-rising flour, omit baking powder and salt.

Heat oven to 350°. Grease a baking pan, 9 × 9 × 2 inches. Beat eggs until light and lemon colored. Beat in sugar and vanilla thoroughly. Blend in flour, baking powder and salt, then stir in dates and nuts. Spread in the pan.

Bake 25 to 30 minutes. Cool and cut into squares. If you like, roll the squares in confectioners' sugar.

16 SQUARES.

PLANTATION FRUIT BARS

½ cup sugar
¼ cup shortening
1 egg
½ cup molasses
½ cup milk
2 cups all-purpose flour*
1½ teaspoons baking powder
½ teaspoon salt
¼ teaspoon soda
1½ cups raisins or cut-up dates
1 cup chopped nuts
Lemon Glaze (right)

*If using self-rising flour, omit baking powder and salt.

Heat oven to 350°. Grease a baking pan, 13 × 9 × 2 inches. Mix thoroughly sugar, shortening, egg and molasses. Blend in remaining ingredients except the glaze. Spread in the pan.

Bake 30 minutes or until a wooden pick inserted in center comes out clean. Cool; spread with Lemon Glaze. Cut into bars, about 3 × 1 inch.

32 BARS.

LEMON GLAZE

2 tablespoons butter or
   margarine
¼ teaspoon grated lemon peel
1 cup confectioners' sugar
1 to 2 tablespoons lemon juice

Melt butter in a small saucepan. Blend in lemon peel and sugar. Stir in lemon juice, 1 tablespoon at a time, until glaze is of spreading consistency.

MARZIPAN COOKIES

1 cup butter or margarine,
   softened
½ cup sugar
2½ cups all-purpose flour*
½ to 1 teaspoon almond extract
   Food color

*Do not use self-rising flour in this recipe.

Cream the butter and sugar. Stir in flour and almond extract until the mixture looks like meal. Divide the dough into 3 equal parts. Color each part and make some of the shapes as directed below. Place cookies on an ungreased baking sheet and chill 30 minutes. Heat oven to 300°. Bake 30 minutes or until set but not brown.

ABOUT 4 DOZEN COOKIES.

ORANGE DOUGH

Apricots: Shape into small balls; crease. Use cloves for stems. Brush on diluted red food color.

Oranges: Shape into small balls; use cloves for blossom ends. For texture, prick with blunt end of a wooden pick.

YELLOW DOUGH

Bananas: Taper and curve 3-inch rolls. Paint on characteristic markings with green food color.

Pears: Make pear shapes; use stick cinnamon for stems. Add "blush" with diluted red food color.

RED DOUGH

Apples: Shape into small balls. Use stick cinnamon for stems, cloves for blossoms. Brush with diluted red food color.

Strawberries: Make heart shapes; roll in red sugar. Use green wooden picks for stems.

GREEN DOUGH

Green Peas: Make 2-inch flat rounds. Divide level teaspoonfuls of dough into 3 or 4 parts and shape into small balls. Place 3 or 4 balls in the center of each round; bring dough up and around.

Green Apples: Shape as directed for Red Apples.

A festival of cookie marzipan fruits—colorful, delicious and well worth the time and care to make them. These shapely sweets add elegance to an afternoon tea and an extra touch of fun to a happy holiday.

1. Add a fresh-looking blush to pears, apricots and apples with diluted red food color. Brush it on before baking.

2. Use small pieces of green wooden picks for the strawberry stems. For even more realism, use bits of green dough for hulls.

CANDY CANES

½ cup butter or margarine, softened
½ cup shortening
1 cup confectioners' sugar
1 egg
1½ teaspoons almond extract
1 teaspoon vanilla
2½ cups all-purpose flour*
1 teaspoon salt
½ teaspoon red food color
½ cup crushed peppermint candy
½ cup granulated sugar

*If using self-rising flour, omit salt. If using quick-mixing flour, stir 2 tablespoons milk into the butter mixture.

Heat oven to 375°. Mix thoroughly butter, shortening, confectioners' sugar, egg, almond extract and vanilla. Blend in flour and salt. Divide the dough in half and blend food color into one half.

For each candy cane, shape 1 teaspoon of dough from each half into a 4-inch rope. (For smooth, even ropes, roll the dough back and forth on a lightly floured board.) Place the ropes side by side and press together lightly; twist. Place on a greased baking sheet and curve the top of each twist to form the handle of the cane.

Bake about 9 minutes or until set and very light brown. Mix candy and granulated sugar; sprinkle on the hot cookies and remove from the baking sheet.

ABOUT 4 DOZEN COOKIES.

Start a new Christmas tradition in your house with these cheery cookie canes. For the best shape and easiest twisting, press the ropes together lightly.

RUSSIAN TEACAKES

1 cup butter or margarine, softened
½ cup confectioners' sugar
1 teaspoon vanilla
2¼ cups all-purpose flour*
¼ teaspoon salt
¾ cup finely chopped nuts

*Do not use self-rising flour in this recipe.

Heat oven to 400°. Mix thoroughly butter, sugar and vanilla. Work in flour, salt and nuts until the dough holds together. Shape the dough into 1-inch balls and place them on an ungreased baking sheet.

Bake 10 to 12 minutes or until set but not brown. While warm, roll in confectioners' sugar. Cool and roll in sugar again.

ABOUT 4 DOZEN COOKIES.

BONBON COOKIES

½ cup butter or margarine, softened
¾ cup confectioners' sugar
1 tablespoon vanilla
Food color, if desired
1½ cups all-purpose flour*
⅛ teaspoon salt
Dates, nuts, semisweet chocolate pieces and candied or maraschino cherries
Icing (below)

*Do not use self-rising flour in this recipe.

Heat oven to 350°. Mix thoroughly butter, sugar, vanilla and a few drops of the food color. Work in flour and salt until the dough holds together. (If the dough is too dry, mix in 1 to 2 tablespoons light cream.)

Mold the dough by tablespoonfuls around a date, nut, chocolate piece or cherry. Place about 1 inch apart on an ungreased baking sheet. Bake 12 to 15 minutes or until set but not brown. Cool. Dip the tops of the cookies into the icing. Cookies can be decorated with coconut, chopped nuts, colored sugar, chocolate pieces or chocolate shot.

ABOUT 2 DOZEN COOKIES.

ICING

Mix 1 cup confectioners' sugar, 2½ tablespoons light cream and 1 teaspoon vanilla until smooth. If desired, stir in a few drops of food color.

DELUXE SUGAR COOKIES

1 cup butter or margarine, softened
1½ cups confectioners' sugar
1 egg
1 teaspoon vanilla
½ teaspoon almond extract
2½ cups all-purpose flour*
1 teaspoon soda
1 teaspoon cream of tartar
Granulated or colored sugar

*If using self-rising flour, omit soda and cream of tartar.

Mix thoroughly butter, confectioners' sugar, egg, vanilla and almond extract. Blend in remaining ingredients except the granulated sugar. Cover the dough and chill 2 to 3 hours.

Heat oven to 375°. Divide the dough in half. Roll each half about ⅛ inch thick on a lightly floured cloth-covered board. Cut into desired shapes and sprinkle with granulated sugar. Place on a lightly greased baking sheet. Bake 7 to 8 minutes or until light brown on the edges. Immediately remove the cookies from the baking sheet.

ABOUT 5 DOZEN COOKIES.

MORAVIAN GINGER COOKIES

⅓ cup molasses
¼ cup shortening
2 tablespoons brown sugar
1¼ cups all-purpose flour*
½ teaspoon salt
¼ teaspoon soda
¼ teaspoon baking powder
¼ teaspoon each cinnamon, ginger and cloves
Dash each of nutmeg and allspice
Easy Creamy Icing (below)

*If using self-rising flour, omit salt, soda and baking powder.

Mix thoroughly molasses, shortening and brown sugar. Blend in remaining ingredients except the icing. Cover the dough and chill at least 4 hours.

Heat oven to 375°. Roll the dough paper thin, about 1/16 inch thick, on a lightly floured cloth-covered board. Cut into desired shapes and place about ½ inch apart on an ungreased baking sheet. Bake 5 to 8 minutes or until set. Immediately remove the cookies from the baking sheet. Cool; frost with Easy Creamy Icing.

ABOUT 5 DOZEN COOKIES.

EASY CREAMY ICING

Mix 1 cup confectioners' sugar, ¼ teaspoon salt, ½ teaspoon vanilla and about 1½ tablespoons light cream until the icing is smooth and of spreading consistency. Tint the icing with a few drops of food color if you like.

JUMBO MOLASSES COOKIES

½ cup shortening
1 cup sugar
1 cup dark molasses
½ cup water
4 cups all-purpose flour*
1½ teaspoons salt
1 teaspoon soda
1½ teaspoons ginger
½ teaspoon cloves
½ teaspoon nutmeg
¼ teaspoon allspice

*If using self-rising flour, omit salt and soda.

Mix thoroughly shortening and sugar. Blend in the remaining ingredients. Cover and chill the dough at least 3 hours.

Heat oven to 375°. Roll the dough ¼ inch thick on a lightly floured cloth-covered board and cut into 3-inch circles. Sprinkle with sugar and place on a well-greased baking sheet. Bake 10 to 12 minutes. Let the cookies cool on the baking sheet about 2 minutes, then remove to a wire rack to cool completely.

ABOUT 3½ DOZEN COOKIES.

CREAM WAFERS

1 cup soft butter
⅓ cup whipping cream
2 cups all-purpose flour
Granulated sugar
Creamy Filling (below)

Mix thoroughly butter, whipping cream and flour. Cover the dough and chill at least 1 hour.

Heat oven to 375°. Using about a third of the dough at a time, roll ⅛ inch thick on a lightly floured cloth-covered board and cut into 1½-inch rounds. With a spatula, transfer the rounds onto a piece of heavily sugared waxed paper. Turn to coat both sides with sugar.

Place the rounds on an ungreased baking sheet and prick each several times with a fork. Bake 7 to 9 minutes or just until set but not brown. Cool; put cookies together in pairs with Creamy Filling.

ABOUT 5 DOZEN COOKIES.

CREAMY FILLING

Mix ¼ cup soft butter, ¾ cup confectioners' sugar and 1 teaspoon vanilla until smooth and fluffy. Tint with food color. If necessary, add a few drops of water for proper spreading consistency.

1 cup shortening (part soft
  butter)
1½ cups brown sugar (packed)
2 eggs
2 teaspoons vanilla
3 cups all-purpose flour*
1 teaspoon salt
½ teaspoon soda
2 cups salted peanuts

*If using self-rising flour, omit salt and soda.

SALTED PEANUT CRISPS

Heat oven to 375°. Mix thoroughly shortening, brown sugar, eggs and vanilla. Stir in the remaining ingredients.

Drop the dough by rounded teaspoonfuls about 2 inches apart onto a lightly greased baking sheet. Flatten dough with the bottom of a glass that's been greased and dipped in sugar. Bake 8 to 10 minutes or until golden brown. Immediately remove the cookies from the baking sheet.

ABOUT 6 DOZEN COOKIES.

VARIATION

Chocolate Chip Peanut Crisps: Stir in 1 package (6 ounces) semisweet chocolate pieces with the salted peanuts.

1 cup raisins
1 cup water
¾ cup shortening
1½ cups sugar
2 eggs
1 teaspoon vanilla
2½ cups all-purpose flour*
1 teaspoon soda
1 teaspoon salt
1 teaspoon cinnamon
½ teaspoon baking powder
½ teaspoon cloves
2 cups oats
½ cup chopped nuts

*If using self-rising flour, omit soda, salt and baking powder.

OLD-FASHIONED OATMEAL COOKIES

Simmer raisins and water over medium heat until the raisins are plump, about 15 minutes. Drain raisins, reserving the liquid. Add enough water to the reserved liquid to measure ½ cup.

Heat oven to 400°. Mix thoroughly shortening, sugar, eggs and vanilla. Blend in the reserved raisin liquid. Stir in the remaining ingredients.

Drop the dough by rounded teaspoonfuls about 2 inches apart onto an ungreased baking sheet. Bake 8 to 10 minutes or until light brown. Immediately remove the cookies from the baking sheet.

ABOUT 6½ DOZEN COOKIES.

PEANUT BUTTER COOKIES

½ cup shortening (half butter
  or margarine, softened)
½ cup creamy or chunk-style
  peanut butter
½ cup granulated sugar
½ cup brown sugar (packed)
1 egg
1¼ cups all-purpose flour*
¾ teaspoon soda
½ teaspoon baking powder
¼ teaspoon salt

*If using self-rising flour, omit soda, baking powder
and salt.

Mix thoroughly shortening, peanut butter, granulated sugar, brown sugar and egg. Blend in the remaining ingredients. Cover and chill about 1 hour.

Heat oven to 375°. Shape the dough into 1-inch balls and place them 3 inches apart on a lightly greased baking sheet. Dip a fork in flour or sugar and press on each ball in a crisscross pattern to flatten to about 2 inches. Bake 10 to 12 minutes or until set but not hard. Immediately remove the cookies from the baking sheet.

ABOUT 3 DOZEN COOKIES.

VARIATION

Peanut Butter Thumbprints: Roll balls of dough in ½ cup finely chopped nuts. Place 2 inches apart on a lightly greased baking sheet. Press thumb in center of each ball. Bake 10 to 12 minutes or just until set. Fill thumbprints with jelly.

SNICKERDOODLES

½ cup butter or margarine,
  softened
½ cup shortening
1½ cups sugar
2 eggs
2¾ cups all-purpose flour*
2 teaspoons cream of tartar
1 teaspoon soda
¼ teaspoon salt
2 tablespoons sugar
2 teaspoons cinnamon

*If using self-rising flour, omit cream of tartar,
soda and salt.

Heat oven to 400°. Mix thoroughly butter, shortening, 1½ cups sugar and the eggs. Blend in flour, cream of tartar, soda and salt. Shape the dough by rounded teaspoonfuls into balls. (Try to make them the size of small walnuts.)

Mix 2 tablespoons sugar and the cinnamon. Roll the balls in the sugar-cinnamon mixture and place them about 2 inches apart on an ungreased baking sheet. Bake 8 to 10 minutes or until set. (The cookies puff up first, then flatten out.) Immediately remove the cookies from the baking sheet.

ABOUT 6 DOZEN COOKIES.

BROWN SUGAR FRUIT DROPS

1 cup shortening
2 cups brown sugar (packed)
2 eggs
½ cup buttermilk or water
3½ cups all-purpose flour*
1 teaspoon soda
1 teaspoon salt
1½ cups broken pecans
2 cups candied cherries, cut into halves
2 cups cut-up dates

*If using self-rising flour, omit soda and salt.

Mix thoroughly shortening, brown sugar, eggs and buttermilk. Stir in the remaining ingredients.

Heat oven to 400°. Drop the dough by rounded teaspoonfuls about 2 inches apart onto a lightly greased baking sheet. If you like, press a pecan half on each cookie. Bake 8 to 10 minutes or until almost no impression remains when touched lightly with a finger. Immediately remove the cookies from the baking sheet.

ABOUT 6 DOZEN COOKIES.

CHERRY ALMOND MACAROONS

1¼ cups diced roasted almonds
¾ cup sugar
3 egg whites
¼ cup chopped maraschino cherries, well drained

Chop nuts coarsely by hand or in a nut grinder. Combine nuts, sugar and egg whites in a saucepan. Cook over medium heat, stirring constantly, 6 to 8 minutes or until a path remains when a spoon is drawn through the mixture. Remove from heat and stir in cherries.

Heat oven to 300°. Drop the dough by rounded teaspoonfuls about 1 inch apart onto a lightly greased and floured baking sheet. Let stand at room temperature until cool to insure rounded cookies. Bake about 20 minutes or until light brown. Immediately remove the cookies from the baking sheet.

ABOUT 1½ DOZEN COOKIES.

EASY FILLED COOKIES

Date Filling (below) or Pineapple-
Cherry Filling (below)
1 cup shortening
2 cups brown sugar (packed)
2 eggs
½ cup water or buttermilk
1 teaspoon vanilla
3½ cups all-purpose flour*
1 teaspoon salt
1 teaspoon soda
⅛ teaspoon cinnamon

*If using self-rising flour, omit salt and soda.

Forget about all the rolling and
cutting usually associated with
filled cookies. We devised a quick
and easy method, like making a
triple-decker drop cookie. A spoon-
ful of dough, a dollop of filling
and then a topping of dough. They
all bake together, and a bit of the
filling peeks out here and there—
just the way you remember those
good old-fashioned cookie-jar
favorites.

Be sure to vary the filling from time
to time, or make half the batch
with one filling and half with
another. Raisin, date-nut, mince-
meat or candied fruit are all good
centerings.

Prepare the filling. Heat oven to 400°. Mix thoroughly shortening, brown sugar and eggs. Stir in
water and vanilla, then blend in the remaining
ingredients.

Drop the dough by teaspoonfuls about 2 inches
apart onto an ungreased baking sheet. Place ½
teaspoon filling on each teaspoonful of dough and
cover with ½ teaspoon dough. Bake 10 to 12 minutes. Immediately remove the cookies from the
baking sheet.

ABOUT 5½ DOZEN COOKIES.

DATE FILLING

2 cups finely cut-up dates
¾ cup sugar
¾ cup water
½ cup chopped nuts

Combine dates, sugar and water in a saucepan.
Cook, stirring constantly, until the mixture thickens. Stir in nuts. Cool.

PINEAPPLE-CHERRY FILLING

1 can (8¼ ounces) crushed
pineapple (1 cup)
¼ cup chopped candied or
maraschino cherries
½ cup sugar
½ cup chopped nuts

Combine pineapple (with syrup), cherries and
sugar in a saucepan. Cook, stirring constantly, until the mixture thickens. Stir in nuts. Cool.

Pies

Pies

Often as not, a woman's reputation as a good cook is based on her pies. And fair or not, the challenge is a delectable one. To help you meet it, and beat it, we've culled the runaway winners from our collection of first-prize pies.

To begin at the beginning, we've placed our perfect-every-time pastry recipe on the very next page. And with it you'll find all the pointers that help to smooth out potential trouble spots.

Then, on to the fillings. For a memorable homey pie there's French Apple, which begins with the classic apple recipe but adds a crunchy crumb topping. And remember Applescotch? It starts with apples pre-cooked in a brown sugar syrup. We go on to follow the seasons with other fruit and berry beauties. There's Rhubarb Custard for spring. Fresh Blueberry for summer—bubbly under its lattice topping. For autumn's masterpiece, we offer the deep-purple magic of Concord Grape Pie, a once-a-year celebration in our own Kitchens.

How about sure-fire pie surprises for party times? Try the spectacular Mile-High Lemon Pie or our two-tiered Chocolate Nesselrode. Frosty Pumpkin is a perfect choice for do-ahead—and we know that many of you rely on it for those big days when the oven's tied up with turkey. For two favorite flavors in one luscious pie, double your pleasure with our Chocolate Pecan. And for a dream in a meringue shell, show off a little with Divine Lime Pie.

Pick out a favorite. Pick up the gauntlet. Do a little something today for your reputation as a good cook.

On the preceding pages:
Applescotch Pie,
Frosty Pumpkin Pie,
Mile-high Lemon Pie,
Chocolate Pecan Pie,
Banana Cream Pie

PASTRY

FOR 9-INCH ONE-CRUST PIE

1 cup all-purpose flour*
½ teaspoon salt
⅓ cup plus 1 tablespoon shortening
2 to 3 tablespoons cold water

FOR 9-INCH TWO-CRUST PIE

2 cups all-purpose flour*
1 teaspoon salt
⅔ cup plus 2 tablespoons shortening
4 to 5 tablespoons cold water

*If using self-rising flour, omit salt. Pie crusts made with self-rising flour differ in flavor and texture from those made with plain flour.

The proof of the pie is in its pastry. Get your pie-time off to a perfect start with these pointers:

1. Before you start rolling the dough, cover the board with a pastry cloth and the rolling pin with a stockinet. Sprinkle both with flour and rub it in well.

2. Roll the dough lightly, always working from the center to the outer edge. Roll evenly in all directions, but never back and forth. Lift the pin as you near the edge to keep the dough from becoming too thin.

3. As you roll, keep the outer edge in a circular shape by pushing in gently with slightly cupped hands.

4. To prevent sticking, lift the pastry from time to time. And, when necessary, rub a little more flour into the cloth and stockinet.

Measure flour and salt into a bowl. Cut in shortening thoroughly with a pastry blender. (The particles should be the size of tiny peas.) Sprinkle in the water, 1 tablespoon at a time, tossing with a fork until all flour is moistened and dough almost cleans the side of the bowl (1 to 2 teaspoons water can be added if needed).

Gather the dough into a ball, then shape into a flattened round on a lightly floured cloth-covered board. (For a Two-crust Pie, divide the dough in half and shape into 2 flattened rounds.) Roll the dough 2 inches larger all around than the inverted pie pan.

Fold the pastry into quarters; unfold and ease into the pan, gently pressing toward the center with your fingertips. (This procedure helps prevent the dough from stretching which would eventually cause skrinkage.)

For One-crust Pie: Trim the overhanging edge of pastry 1 inch from rim of pan. Fold and roll pastry under, even with the pan, and flute. Fill and bake as directed in recipe.

For Baked Pie Shell: Prick bottom and side thoroughly with a fork. Bake in a 475° oven 8 to 10 minutes.

For Two-crust Pie: Pour desired filling into the pastry-lined pie pan. Trim the overhanging edge of pastry ½ inch from rim of pan. Roll the second round of dough. Fold into quarters and cut slits. (The slits allow steam to escape while the pie bakes.) Place over the filling and unfold. Trim the overhanging edge of pastry 1 inch from rim of pan. Fold and roll the top edge under the lower edge, pressing on the rim to seal; flute.

APPLESCOTCH PIE

5 cups thinly sliced pared tart
  apples (about 4 medium)
1 cup brown sugar (packed)
¼ cup water
1 tablespoon lemon juice
¼ cup all-purpose flour
2 tablespoons granulated sugar
¾ teaspoon salt
1 teaspoon vanilla
3 tablespoons butter or margarine
  Pastry for 9-inch Two-crust Pie
  (page 123)

Combine apple slices, brown sugar, water and lemon juice in a saucepan. Cover and cook over medium heat until the apples are *just* tender, about 5 minutes.

Mix flour, granulated sugar and salt and stir into apple mixture. Cook, stirring constantly, until the syrup thickens—about 2 minutes. Remove from heat and stir in vanilla and butter.

Heat oven to 425°. Prepare the pastry. Turn the apple mixture into the pastry-lined pie pan. Cover with top crust which has slits cut in it; seal and flute. Cover the edge with a 2- to 3-inch strip of aluminum foil to prevent excessive browning; remove the foil for the last 15 minutes of baking. Bake 40 to 45 minutes or until the crust is golden brown.

FRENCH APPLE PIE

Pastry for 9-inch One-crust Pie
  (page 123)
¾ cup sugar
¼ cup all-purpose flour
½ teaspoon nutmeg
½ teaspoon cinnamon
  Dash of salt
6 cups thinly sliced pared
  apples (about 5 medium)
  Crumb Topping (below)

Heat oven to 425°. Prepare the pastry. Stir together sugar, flour, nutmeg, cinnamon and salt; mix lightly with the apples. Pour into the pastry-lined pie pan and sprinkle with Crumb Topping.

Cover the edge with a 2- to 3-inch strip of aluminum foil to prevent excessive browning; remove the foil for the last 15 minutes of baking. Bake 40 to 50 minutes. If the topping is browning too quickly, cover it with foil for the last 15 minutes of baking.

CRUMB TOPPING

Mix 1 cup all-purpose flour,* ½ cup firm butter or margarine and ½ cup brown sugar (packed) with a fork or pastry blender until crumbly.

*Do not use self-rising flour in this recipe.

CHERRY PIE

Pastry for 9-inch Two-crust Pie
(page 123)
1⅓ cups sugar
⅓ cup all-purpose flour
2 cans (16 ounces each) pitted
red tart cherries, drained
¼ teaspoon almond extract
2 tablespoons butter or margarine

Heat oven to 425°. Prepare the pastry. Stir together sugar and flour and mix lightly with the cherries. Pour into the pastry-lined pie pan. Sprinkle fruit with almond extract and dot with butter.

Cover with top crust which has slits cut in it; seal and flute. Cover edge with 2- to 3-inch strip of aluminum foil to prevent excessive browning; remove the foil for the last 15 minutes of baking. Bake 35 to 45 minutes or until the crust is golden brown and the juice begins to bubble through the slits. Serve slightly warm.

VARIATIONS

Fresh Cherry Pie: Substitute 4 cups fresh red tart cherries, washed and pitted, for the canned cherries.

Frozen Cherry Pie: Substitute 2 cans (20 ounces each) frozen pitted red tart cherries, thawed and drained, for the canned cherries; decrease sugar to ½ cup.

CHERRY-BANANA PIE

9-inch Baked Pie Shell
(page 123)
1 can (16 ounces) pitted red
tart cherries
1 cup sugar
3 tablespoons cornstarch
1 tablespoon butter or margarine
½ teaspoon cinnamon
1 teaspoon almond extract
2 medium bananas

Bake the pie shell. Cool.

Combine cherries (with liquid), sugar and cornstarch in a saucepan. Cook over medium heat, stirring constantly, until the mixture thickens and boils. Boil and stir 1 minute. Stir in butter and cool.

Stir in cinnamon and almond extract. Slice bananas into the pie shell. Pour the cherry filling over the banana slices and chill at least 3 hours or until set. Garnish with whipped cream and banana slices.

FRESH BERRY PIE

Lattice Top Pastry (below)
1 cup sugar
⅓ cup all-purpose flour
4 cups fresh berries (raspberries, blackberries, boysenberries, loganberries)
1 tablespoon lemon juice
2 tablespoons butter or margarine

Heat oven to 425°. Prepare the pastry. Stir together sugar and flour and mix lightly with the berries. Pour into the pastry-lined pie pan. Sprinkle with lemon juice and dot with butter.

Cover with lattice top; seal and flute. Cover the edge with a 2- to 3-inch strip of aluminum foil to prevent excessive browning; remove the foil for the last 15 minutes of baking. Bake 35 to 45 minutes or until the crust is golden brown. Serve warm.

LATTICE TOP PASTRY

Prepare pastry as directed for 9-inch Two-crust Pie (page 123) except—leave a 1-inch overhang on the lower crust. After rolling the circle for the top crust, cut into 10 strips, about ½ inch wide. For fancy edges, cut the strips with a pastry wheel.

Place 5 strips about 1 inch apart across the filling in the pie pan. Weave a cross-strip through the center by first folding back every other one of the original strips. Continue weaving until the lattice is complete, folding back the alternate strips each time a cross-strip is added. (Too time-pressed to weave? Simply lay the second set of strips across the first set.) Trim ends of strips.

Fold the trimmed edge of the lower crust over the ends of the strips, building up a high edge. (A juicy fruit pie is more likely to bubble over when topped by a lattice than when the juices are held in by a top crust—so be sure to build up a high edge.) Seal and flute.

VARIATION

Blueberry Pie: Decrease sugar to ½ cup, add ½ teaspoon cinnamon and use 4 cups fresh blueberries.

There's nothing quite like a fresh berry pie—for dessert or a snack. Our beauty abounds with juicy boysenberries, but use whatever berry is in season and suits your taste.

1. The simplest way to start the lattice is to center the first strip; then space the others equally on either side.

2. For an even lattice, fold back every other one of the original strips; then weave cross-strips, handling the center one first.

PEACH MELBA PIE

Pastry for 9-inch Two-crust Pie
(page 123)
¼ cup sugar
2 tablespoons cornstarch
2 packages (12 ounces each)
frozen peach slices, thawed
and drained (reserve ¼ cup
syrup)
1 package (10 ounces) frozen
red raspberries, thawed and
drained (reserve ½ cup syrup for
the sauce)
1 tablespoon butter
Vanilla ice cream
Melba Sauce (below)

Heat oven to 425°. Prepare the pastry. Combine sugar, cornstarch and reserved peach syrup in a saucepan. Cook over medium heat, stirring constantly, until the mixture thickens and boils. Boil and stir 1 minute. Pour the hot syrup over peach slices.

Spread raspberries evenly in the pastry-lined pie pan; cover with the peach mixture and dot with butter.

Cover with top crust which has slits cut in it; seal and flute. Cover the edge with a 2- to 3-inch strip of aluminum foil to prevent excessive browning; remove the foil for the last 15 minutes of baking. Bake 40 to 45 minutes or until the crust is golden brown. Serve warm, with ice cream and Melba Sauce.

Note: 1 can (29 ounces) plus 1 can (17 ounces) sliced peaches, drained (reserve ¼ cup syrup), can be substituted for the frozen peaches. Increase sugar to ½ cup.

MELBA SAUCE

In a small saucepan, combine 2 teaspoons cornstarch, ¼ cup currant jelly or red raspberry preserves and the ½ cup reserved raspberry syrup. Cook over medium heat, stirring constantly, until the mixture thickens and boils. Boil and stir 1 minute. Cool.

VARIATION

Blushing Peach Pie: Omit the raspberries and Melba Sauce. Stir ¼ cup red cinnamon candies into the hot peach-syrup mixture.

CONCORD GRAPE PIE

5⅓ cups Concord grapes
1⅓ cups sugar
¼ cup all-purpose flour
1½ teaspoons lemon juice
　Dash of salt
　Pastry for 9-inch Two-crust Pie
　(page 123)
1 tablespoon plus 1 teaspoon
　butter or margarine

Remove skins from grapes and set aside. (To remove the skins quickly, simply pinch each grape at the end opposite the stem—the fruit will pop right out.) Heat the grape pulp (without any water) just to boiling. While hot, rub through a strainer to remove seeds. Combine the strained pulp and the skins. Mix sugar and flour. Stir the sugar mixture, lemon juice and salt into the grape mixture.

Heat oven to 425°. Prepare the pastry. Pour the grape mixture into the pastry-lined pie pan and dot with butter. Cover with top crust which has slits cut in it; seal and flute. Cover the edge with a 2- to 3-inch strip of aluminum foil to prevent excessive browning; remove the foil for the last 15 minutes of baking. Bake 35 to 45 minutes or until the crust is golden brown and the juice begins to bubble through the slits. Serve warm.

RHUBARB CUSTARD PIE

　Lattice Top Pastry (page 126)
3 eggs
2 cups sugar
3 tablespoons milk
¼ cup all-purpose flour
½ teaspoon nutmeg
4 cups diced rhubarb
1 tablespoon butter or margarine

Heat oven to 400°. Prepare the pastry. Beat eggs slightly and stir in the remaining ingredients. Pour into the pastry-lined pie pan and dot with butter.

Cover with lattice top. Cover edge with a 2- to 3-inch strip of aluminum foil to prevent excessive browning; remove the foil for the last 15 minutes of baking. Bake 50 to 60 minutes or until the crust is golden brown. Serve warm.

2 cups all-purpose flour*
⅔ cup shredded sharp natural
    Cheddar cheese
1 teaspoon salt
⅔ cup plus 2 tablespoons
    shortening
¼ cup water
    Clear Orange Sauce (below)
1 pint fresh strawberries
    (reserve 7 whole berries),
    cut into halves
3 medium peaches, peeled and
    sliced
1½ cups seedless green grapes
1 medium banana, cut into ⅛-inch
    slices
2 tablespoons sugar
    Sweetened whipped cream

*If using self-rising flour, omit salt. Pie crusts made
with self-rising flour differ in flavor and texture from
those made with plain flour.

A luscious looking pie that swings
with the seasons. This summer
spectacular can become a winter
wonder by substituting canned and
frozen fruits for the fresh. Or
switch to any available fruit that
pleases your palate. It's an ideal
centerpiece-dessert for a bridge
lunch; a hearty and healthful finish
for a light supper.

And it's adaptable in still another
way. If you don't have a pizza pan,
the pastry circle can be baked
just as successfully on an ungreased
baking sheet. Just remember to
flute the edge.

FRUIT PLATTER PIE

Heat oven to 475°. Measure flour, cheese and salt into a bowl. Cut in shortening thoroughly with a pastry blender. Sprinkle in water, 1 tablespoon at a time, mixing until all flour is moistened and dough almost cleans the side of the bowl (1 to 2 teaspoons water can be added if needed).

Gather the dough into a ball and roll into a 15-inch circle on a lightly floured cloth-covered board. Roll the circle onto the rolling pin, then unroll on a 14-inch pizza pan. Fold under ½ inch of dough around edge and pinch or pleat edge. Prick bottom and side of pastry. Bake 8 to 10 minutes. Cool.

Prepare Clear Orange Sauce. Arrange strawberry halves around the edge of pastry shell. Arrange peach slices in a circle next to strawberries. Mound grapes in a circle next to peach slices, then a circle of overlapping banana slices. Place reserved berries in the center. Sprinkle the fruits with sugar and spoon on some of the orange sauce. Serve with whipped cream and the remaining sauce.

12 TO 14 SERVINGS.

CLEAR ORANGE SAUCE

1 cup sugar
¼ teaspoon salt
2 tablespoons cornstarch
1 cup orange juice
¼ cup lemon juice
¾ cup water
½ teaspoon grated orange peel
½ teaspoon grated lemon peel

Mix sugar, salt and cornstarch in a small saucepan. Stir in orange juice, lemon juice and water. Cook, stirring constantly, until the mixture thickens and boils. Boil and stir 1 minute. Remove from heat and stir in the grated peels. Cool.

BANANA CREAM PIE

9-inch Graham Cracker Crust
(page 139)
⅔ cup sugar
¼ cup cornstarch
½ teaspoon salt
3 cups milk
4 egg yolks, slightly beaten
2 tablespoons butter or margarine
1 tablespoon plus 1 teaspoon
vanilla
2 large bananas
Sweetened whipped cream

Bake the Graham Cracker Crust. Cool.

Mix sugar, cornstarch and salt in a saucepan. Blend milk and egg yolks; gradually stir into the sugar mixture. Cook over medium heat, stirring constantly, until the mixture thickens and boils. Boil and stir 1 minute. Remove from heat and blend in butter and vanilla. Press plastic wrap onto filling in saucepan and cool to room temperature.

Slice bananas into the crust, arranging them in a layer about ½ inch deep. Pour the cream filling over banana slices and chill at least 2 hours. Just before serving, top pie with sweetened whipped cream.

CHOCOLATE PECAN PIE

Pastry for 9-inch One-crust Pie
(page 123)
1¼ cups light corn syrup
½ cup sugar
1 bar (4 ounces) sweet cooking
chocolate
½ cup evaporated milk
3 eggs, slightly beaten
1 cup pecan halves

Heat oven to 350°. Prepare the pastry. Combine corn syrup, sugar, chocolate and milk in a saucepan. Heat, stirring constantly, *just* until the chocolate is melted. Gradually stir the hot mixture into eggs, then stir in pecan halves. Pour into the pastry-lined pie pan. Bake 50 to 60 minutes. (Center will appear soft.) Cool. Try this pie topped with sweetened whipped cream or vanilla ice cream.

Note: You'll want to cut this pie into smaller-than-average wedges—it's very rich.

9-inch Baked Pie Shell
(page 123)
1½ cups sugar
⅓ cup plus 1 tablespoon
   cornstarch
1½ cups water
 3 egg yolks, slightly beaten
 3 tablespoons butter or margarine
 2 teaspoons grated lemon peel
½ cup lemon juice
 2 drops yellow food color, if
   desired
   Pie Meringue (below)

There's no mystery to. making a
perfect meringue pie. With a little
care and these clues, the delicate
topping will be light-as-air, high
and golden brown every try.

1. Separate eggs carefully. (It's
easier to do when they're cold.)
Even a speck of yolk can hold down
the peaks.

2. Wait until the egg whites come
to room temperature before beating.
They'll be higher and lighter.

3. Beat in the sugar *gradually*—and
continue beating until it is completely dissolved.

4. Spread the meringue over a *hot*
filling, right to the crust all the
way around.

5. Watch baking time.

6. Dodge drafts; a chill may make
the meringue shrink.

LEMON MERINGUE PIE

Bake the pie shell. Cool.

Heat oven to 400°. Mix sugar and cornstarch in a
medium saucepan. Gradually stir in water. Cook
over medium heat, stirring constantly, until the
mixture thickens and boils. Boil and stir 1 minute.

Gradually stir at least half the hot mixture into the
egg yolks; blend into the hot mixture in the saucepan. Boil and stir 1 minute. Remove from heat and
stir in butter, lemon peel, lemon juice and food
color. Immediately pour into the pie shell.

Heap the meringue onto the hot pie filling and
spread over the filling, carefully sealing the meringue
to the edge of the crust to prevent shrinking or
weeping. Bake about 10 minutes or until a delicate
brown. Cool gradually to prevent shrinking.

PIE MERINGUE
 3 egg whites
¼ teaspoon cream of tartar
 6 tablespoons sugar
½ teaspoon vanilla

Beat egg whites and cream of tartar until foamy.
Beat in sugar, 1 tablespoon at a time, and continue
beating until stiff and glossy. *Do not underbeat.* Beat
in vanilla.

VARIATION

Lime Meringue Pie: Decrease cornstarch to ⅓ cup and
omit butter. Substitute 2 teaspoons grated lime
peel and ¼ cup lime juice for the lemon peel and
juice and green food color for the yellow.

Lemon Meringue Pie

COCONUT CHIFFON PIE

9- inch Baked Pie Shell
  (page 123)
½ cup sugar
¼ cup all-purpose flour
1 envelope unflavored gelatin
½ teaspoon salt
1¾ cups milk
¾ teaspoon vanilla
¼ teaspoon almond extract
3 egg whites
¼ teaspoon cream of tartar
½ cup sugar
½ cup chilled whipping cream
1 cup shredded coconut
  Sweetened strawberries or
  raspberries

Bake the pie shell. Cool.

Mix ½ cup sugar, the flour, gelatin and salt in a saucepan. Gradually stir in milk. Heat *just* to boiling, stirring constantly. Place the pan in a bowl of ice and water or chill in refrigerator, stirring occasionally, until the mixture mounds slightly when dropped from a spoon. Stir in vanilla and almond extract.

Beat egg whites and cream of tartar until foamy. Beat in ½ cup sugar, 1 tablespoon at a time, and continue beating until stiff and glossy. *Do not underbeat.* Fold in the gelatin mixture.

In a chilled bowl, beat whipping cream until stiff. Fold whipped cream and coconut into the meringue mixture. Pile into the pie shell and chill 3 hours or until set. Serve with sweetened berries.

RASPBERRY CHIFFON PIE

9- inch Baked Pie Shell
  (page 123)
⅔ cup sugar
1 envelope unflavored gelatin
1 pint fresh raspberries, crushed
3 egg whites
¼ teaspoon cream of tartar
⅓ cup sugar
½ cup chilled whipping cream

Bake the pie shell. Cool.

Mix ⅔ cup sugar and the gelatin in a saucepan. Stir in crushed raspberries. Cook over medium heat, stirring constantly, just until the mixture boils. Place the pan in a bowl of ice and water or chill in refrigerator, stirring occasionally, until the mixture mounds slightly when dropped from a spoon.

Beat egg whites and cream of tartar until foamy. Beat in ⅓ cup sugar, 1 tablespoon at a time, and continue beating until stiff and glossy. *Do not underbeat.* Fold in the raspberry mixture.

In a chilled bowl, beat whipping cream until stiff; fold into the raspberry meringue. Pile into the pie shell and chill at least 3 hours or until set.

MILE-HIGH LEMON PIE

9-inch Baked Pie Shell
  (page 123)
1 cup sugar
¼ teaspoon salt
1 envelope unflavored gelatin
8 egg yolks, beaten
½ cup water
½ cup lemon juice
1 tablespoon grated lemon peel
8 egg whites
¼ teaspoon cream of tartar
1 cup sugar

Bake the pie shell. Cool.

Mix 1 cup sugar, the salt and gelatin in a medium saucepan. Blend egg yolks, water and lemon juice and stir into the sugar mixture. Cook over medium heat, stirring constantly, just until the mixture boils. Stir in lemon peel.

Place the pan in a bowl of ice and water or chill in refrigerator, stirring occasionally, until the mixture mounds slightly when dropped from a spoon.

Beat egg whites and cream of tartar until foamy. Beat in 1 cup sugar, 1 tablespoon at a time, and continue beating until stiff and glossy. *Do not underbeat.* Fold in the lemon mixture. Pile into the pie shell and chill at least 3 hours or until set.

CHOCOLATE ANGEL PIE

2 egg whites
¼ teaspoon cream of tartar
½ cup sugar
1 bar (4 ounces) sweet cooking
  chocolate
3 tablespoons hot water
1 teaspoon vanilla
1 cup chilled whipping cream

Heat oven to 275°. Generously butter an 8-inch pie pan. In small mixer bowl, beat egg whites and cream of tartar until foamy. Beat in sugar, 1 tablespoon at a time, and continue beating until stiff and glossy—about 10 minutes. *Do not underbeat.*

Pile into the pie pan, pressing meringue up against the side. Bake 1 hour. Turn off the oven; leave meringue in oven with the door closed 1 hour. Remove from oven and cool.

Melt chocolate in hot water over low heat, stirring constantly. Cool to room temperature. Stir in vanilla. In a chilled bowl, beat whipping cream until stiff, then fold in the chocolate mixture. Pile into the meringue shell and chill at least 12 hours. Garnish with whipped cream, chopped nuts or chocolate curls.

DIVINE LIME PIE

4 egg whites
¼ teaspoon cream of tartar
1 cup sugar
4 egg yolks
¼ teaspoon salt
½ cup sugar
⅓ cup fresh lime juice (2 to 3 limes)
2 to 3 drops green food color
1 cup chilled whipping cream
1 tablespoon grated lime peel

Heat oven to 275°. Generously butter a 9-inch pie pan. In small mixer bowl, beat egg whites and cream of tartar until foamy. Beat in 1 cup sugar, 1 tablespoon at a time, and continue beating until stiff and glossy—about 10 minutes. *Do not underbeat.*

Pile into the pie pan, pressing meringue up against the side. Bake 1 hour. Turn off the oven; leave meringue in oven with the door closed 1 hour. Remove from oven and cool.

Beat egg yolks until light and lemon colored. Stir in salt, ½ cup sugar and the lime juice. Cook over medium heat, stirring constantly, until the mixture thickens—about 5 minutes. Cool and tint with food color.

In a chilled bowl, beat whipping cream until stiff. Fold in the lime mixture and grated lime peel. Pile into the meringue shell and chill at least 4 hours. Garnish with whipped cream and grated lime peel or lime twists.

PINEAPPLE MALLOW PIE

9-inch Graham Cracker Crust (page 139)
32 large or 3 cups miniature marshmallows
1 can (20 ounces) crushed pineapple, drained (reserve ½ cup syrup)
1 cup chilled whipping cream
1 teaspoon vanilla
¼ teaspoon salt

Bake the Graham Cracker Crust. Cool.

Heat marshmallows and reserved pineapple syrup over low heat, stirring constantly, until marshmallows are melted. Chill until thickened.

In a chilled bowl, beat whipping cream until stiff. Stir the marshmallow mixture until blended and fold into the whipped cream. Reserving ½ cup crushed pineapple for a garnish, fold the remaining pineapple, the vanilla and salt into the marshmallow mixture. Pour into the crust and garnish with the reserved pineapple. Chill 2 to 3 hours.

CHOCOLATE NESSELRODE PIE

9-inch Baked Pie Shell
  (page 123)
½ cup sugar
¼ cup cornstarch
1 tablespoon plus 1 teaspoon
  unflavored gelatin
½ teaspoon salt
2 cups milk
6 egg yolks, slightly beaten
1 bar (4 ounces) sweet cooking
  chocolate, grated
1 teaspoon vanilla
½ teaspoon rum flavoring
1 jar (10 ounces) Nesselrode
3 cups chilled whipping cream

Bake the pie shell. Cool.

Mix sugar, cornstarch, gelatin and salt in a saucepan. Blend egg yolks and milk and stir into the sugar mixture. Cook over medium heat, stirring constantly, until the mixture thickens and boils. Boil and stir 1 minute. Pour 1½ cups of this hot mixture into a bowl; set aside and cool.

Reserving 2 tablespoons of the grated chocolate for topping, blend the remaining chocolate and the vanilla into the mixture remaining in the saucepan. Cool.

Line a 9-inch pie pan with waxed paper. Stir rum flavoring and Nesselrode into the plain gelatin mixture. In a chilled bowl, beat 2 cups of the whipping cream until stiff; fold half into the Nesselrode mixture and half into the chocolate mixture. Pour the chocolate mixture into the baked pie shell. Pour the Nesselrode mixture into the waxed paper-lined pan. Chill both until firm.

Just before serving, loosen the edge of the Nesselrode layer with a spatula and invert onto the chocolate filling; remove the waxed paper. In a chilled bowl, beat the remaining whipping cream until stiff and spread over the pie. Sprinkle with the reserved chocolate and serve immediately.

FRENCH STRAWBERRY GLACÉ PIE

9-inch Baked Pie Shell
  (page 123)
6 cups fresh strawberries (about
  1½ quarts)
1 cup sugar
3 tablespoons cornstarch
½ cup water
1 package (3 ounces) cream
  cheese, softened

Bake the pie shell. Cool.

Mash enough strawberries to measure 1 cup. Mix sugar and cornstarch in a saucepan; stir in water and the crushed berries. Cook over medium heat, stirring constantly, until the mixture thickens and boils. Boil and stir 1 minute. Cool.

Beat cream cheese until smooth and spread on the bottom of the baked pie shell. Fill the shell with the remaining berries and pour the cooked berry mixture on top. Chill at least 3 hours or until set. If you like, serve with sweetened whipped cream.

VARIATION

French Raspberry Glacé Pie: Substitute 6 cups fresh raspberries for the strawberries.

FROZEN LEMON PIE

9-inch Graham Cracker Crust
  (page 139)
3 eggs, separated
½ cup sugar
1 cup chilled whipping cream or
  1 envelope (about 1½ ounces)
  whipped topping mix
2 teaspoons grated lemon peel
¼ cup lemon juice

Prepare the Graham Cracker Crust, reserving 2 tablespoons of the crumbs for garnish. Bake and cool.

Beat egg whites until foamy. Beat in sugar, 1 tablespoon at a time, and continue beating until stiff and glossy. Beat egg yolks until thick and fold into the egg whites.

In a chilled bowl, beat whipping cream until stiff. (If using whipped topping mix, prepare as directed on package.) Fold the whipped cream, lemon peel and lemon juice into the egg mixture. Pour into the crust and sprinkle reserved crumbs on top. Freeze until firm, about 8 hours. Remove the pie from the freezer about 15 minutes before serving.

FROZEN CHOCOLATE PIE

9-inch Baked Pie Shell
   (page 123)
1 cup confectioners' sugar
½ cup soft butter
6 squares (1 ounce each)
   semisweet chocolate or 1 package
   (6 ounces) semisweet chocolate
   pieces, melted and cooled
1 teaspoon vanilla
4 eggs
1 cup chilled whipping cream
2 tablespoons confectioners' sugar

Bake the pie shell. Cool.

In a small mixer bowl, blend 1 cup confectioners' sugar and the butter on low speed until fluffy. Blend in chocolate and vanilla. Add eggs, one at a time, beating thoroughly on high speed after each addition. Pour into the pie shell and freeze until firm, about 8 hours. Remove the pie from the freezer about 15 minutes before serving.

In a chilled bowl, beat whipping cream and 2 tablespoons confectioners' sugar until stiff. Pile onto the frozen pie and garnish with chocolate curls.

FROSTY PUMPKIN PIE

9-inch Graham Cracker Crust
   (below)
1 cup canned pumpkin
½ cup brown sugar (packed)
½ teaspoon salt
½ teaspoon cinnamon
½ teaspoon ginger
¼ teaspoon nutmeg
1 quart vanilla ice cream,
   slightly softened
   Sweetened whipped cream
   Walnut halves or candy corn

Bake the Graham Cracker Crust. Cool.

Beat pumpkin, sugar, salt and spices until smooth. Stir in ice cream. Pour into the crust and freeze at least 8 hours. For easy cutting, remove the pie from the freezer 15 minutes before serving. Garnish with sweetened whipped cream and the walnut halves.

9-INCH GRAHAM CRACKER CRUST

1½ cups graham cracker crumbs
   (about 20 crackers)
 3 tablespoons sugar
⅓ cup butter or margarine, melted

Heat oven to 350°. Mix cracker crumbs, sugar and butter. (If desired, reserve 2 to 3 tablespoons crumb mixture to sprinkle on pie.) Press the remaining mixture firmly and evenly against bottom and side of a 9-inch pie pan. Bake 10 minutes. Cool.

Desserts

Desserts

"I'm saving the best till last." That's what all of us used to say, and think, about desserts—which always were served as the final course at lunch and dinner. But times change. Today, the well-chosen dessert goes anywhere you want it to. What's more, it's practically become a way of entertaining.

So...who says you can't take Fresh Fruit Cobbler to breakfast on a wintry morning? Why not feature Strawberry Shortcake for a weekend brunch? It's really the very wholesome (and nutritious) bread, fruit and milk in an unexpected guise. Give some thought to Cherry-Berries on a Cloud at a dessert-bridge, tiny Cream Puffs for a baby shower, Company Cheesecake for a "drop by for coffee and cake" evening. Then go it alone. Dream up your own dessert doings for warm-from-the-oven, old-fashioned charmers like Peach Dumplings, Gingerbread, Steamed Plum Pudding (festively aflame—if that's your style).

We still like desserts in their accustomed place. For instance, try Mocha Brownie Torte as the fancy finish to a dressy dinner. Or how about a speeded-up version of the elegant Pots de Crème au Chocolat? Napoleons and Jam Tartlets are pretty pleasers, too. In fact, they're our own answer to French pastry, but supremely simplified and guaranteed to succeed.

Sweetest of all, perhaps—many of these favorites can be made in advance, and some go modern with mixes. Fitting gestures, you might say, to the liberated role of desserts today. And to the woman who makes them.

On the preceding pages:
Pots de Crème au Chocolat,
Jam Tartlets, Cream Puffs and Napoleons,
Company Cheesecake,
Mocha Brownie Torte,
Peach Shortcake Parisienne

STRAWBERRY SHORTCAKE

1 quart fresh strawberries
1 cup sugar
2 cups all-purpose flour*
2 tablespoons sugar
3 teaspoons baking powder
1 teaspoon salt
⅓ cup shortening
1 cup milk
    Butter or margarine
    Light cream or sweetened
    whipped cream

*If using self-rising flour, omit baking powder and salt.

Pull a shortcake switch. Use sweetened raspberries or sliced peaches or maybe even a mixed-fruit medley in place of the strawberries.

Slice the strawberries into a bowl. Sprinkle with 1 cup sugar and let stand about 1 hour.

Heat oven to 450°. Measure flour, 2 tablespoons sugar, the baking powder and salt into a bowl. Cut in shortening with a pastry blender until the mixture looks like meal. Stir in milk just until blended. Pat the dough into a greased layer pan, 8 × 1½ inches.

Bake 15 to 20 minutes or until golden brown. Split layer crosswise while hot and spread with butter. Fill and top with the sweetened berries. Serve warm, topped with light cream.

6 TO 8 SERVINGS.

Note: For a crusty shortcake, spread the dough in 2 greased layer pans, 8 × 1½ inches. Dot with butter and bake 12 to 15 minutes.

PEACH SHORTCAKE PARISIENNE

Heat oven to 400°. Prepare Regular Shortcake dough as directed on a package of buttermilk baking mix except—divide the dough in half and roll one half into an 8-inch square. Place in an ungreased baking pan, 8 × 8 × 2 inches. Dot with butter and sprinkle with ¼ cup brown sugar (packed).

Roll the remaining dough into an 8-inch square and place over the square in the pan. Bake 10 to 15 minutes or until golden brown.

Cut the warm shortcake into squares and serve with sweetened whipped cream or dairy sour cream and sliced fresh or frozen (thawed) peaches.

9 SERVINGS.

GINGERBREAD

2¼ cups all-purpose flour*
  or cake flour
⅓ cup sugar
1 cup dark molasses
¾ cup hot water
½ cup shortening
1 egg
1 teaspoon soda
1 teaspoon ginger
1 teaspoon cinnamon
¾ teaspoon salt
  Sweetened whipped cream
  or applesauce

*Do not use self-rising flour in this recipe.

Heat oven to 325°. Grease and flour a baking pan, 9×9×2 inches. Measure all ingredients except the whipped cream into a large mixer bowl. Blend ½ minute on low speed, scraping the bowl constantly. Beat 3 minutes on medium speed, scraping occasionally. Pour into the pan.

Bake 50 minutes or until a wooden pick inserted in center comes out clean. Serve warm with sweetened whipped cream or applesauce.

9 SERVINGS.

WARM CRANBERRY CAKE WITH BUTTER SAUCE

2 cups buttermilk baking mix
½ cup sugar
2 tablespoons shortening, melted
⅓ cup milk
1 egg
2 cups fresh or frozen (thawed) cranberries
  Butter Sauce (below)

This recipe for Butter Sauce is a special favorite. Try it as a warm topping for gingerbread, cottage pudding, date or plum puddings, for spice cake or vanilla ice cream.

Heat oven to 350°. Grease and flour a baking pan, 9×9×2 inches. Mix the baking mix, sugar, shortening, milk and egg. Beat vigorously ½ minute, then fold in the cranberries. Spread the batter in the pan.

Bake about 35 minutes or until the cake is golden brown and a wooden pick inserted in center comes out clean. Serve with warm Butter Sauce.

9 TO 12 SERVINGS.

BUTTER SAUCE

Combine ½ cup butter or margarine, 1 cup sugar and ¾ cup half-and-half in a saucepan. Cook over low heat, stirring constantly, until the mixture is smooth. Add the grated peel of 1 lemon for a tangy flavor.

ABOUT 2 CUPS SAUCE.

PINEAPPLE UPSIDE-DOWN CAKE

2 tablespoons butter or
margarine
⅓ cup brown sugar (packed)
1 can (8¼ ounces) sliced
pineapple, drained
Maraschino cherries
Pecan halves
Velvet Crumb Cake batter

Heat oven to 350°. Melt butter over low heat in a baking pan, 8 × 8 × 2 inches, or a layer pan, 9 × 1½ inches. Sprinkle with brown sugar. Arrange fruit and nuts on the sugar mixture.

Prepare Velvet Crumb Cake batter as directed on a package of buttermilk baking mix. Pour batter over the fruit in the pan.

Bake 35 to 40 minutes or until a wooden pick inserted in center comes out clean. Immediately invert the pan onto a serving plate. Let the pan remain a few minutes so the sugar mixture will drizzle down the sides of the cake. This is especially delicious when served warm, with whipped cream.

9 TO 12 SERVINGS.

MOCHA BROWNIE TORTE

1 package (15.5 ounces)
fudge brownie mix
¼ cup water
2 eggs
½ cup finely chopped nuts
1½ cups chilled whipping
cream or 3 cups frozen
whipped topping*
⅓ cup brown sugar (packed)
1 tablespoon powdered instant
coffee
Shaved chocolate or chocolate
curls

*If using frozen whipped topping, thaw; omit sugar and fold in the instant coffee.

Heat oven to 350°. Grease and flour 2 layer pans, 9 × 1½ inches. Blend brownie mix (dry), water and eggs. Stir in nuts. Spread in the pans and bake 20 minutes. Cool 5 minutes in pans; remove layers from pans and place on wire racks to cool thoroughly.

In a chilled bowl, beat whipping cream until it begins to thicken. Gradually add sugar and coffee; continue beating until stiff. Fill layers with 1 cup of the whipped cream mixture. Frost sides and top with the remaining whipped cream mixture and garnish the top with shaved chocolate. Chill at least 1 hour before serving.

10 TO 12 SERVINGS.

NUT CRACKER SWEET TORTE

6 eggs, separated
½ cup sugar
2 tablespoons salad oil
1 tablespoon rum flavoring
½ cup sugar
¼ cup all-purpose flour*
1¼ teaspoons baking powder
1 teaspoon cinnamon
½ teaspoon cloves
1 cup fine graham cracker crumbs
(about 12 crackers)
1 square (1 ounce) unsweetened
chocolate, grated
1 cup finely chopped nuts
Rum-flavored Whipped Cream
(below)

*If using self-rising flour, decrease baking powder to
1 teaspoon.

Heat oven to 350°. Line the bottoms of 2 layer pans, 8 or 9 × 1½ inches, with aluminum foil. In a large mixer bowl, beat egg whites until foamy. Beat in ½ cup sugar, 1 tablespoon at a time, and continue beating until stiff and glossy.

In a small mixer bowl, blend egg yolks, oil and rum flavoring on low speed. Add ½ cup sugar, the flour, baking powder, cinnamon and cloves; beat 1 minute on medium speed, scraping the bowl occasionally. Fold the egg yolk mixture into the egg whites. Fold in crumbs, chocolate and nuts. Pour into the pans.

Bake 30 to 35 minutes or until the top springs back when touched lightly with finger. Immediately invert each pan, resting the rim on the edges of 2 inverted pans. Cool completely.

Loosen the edges of the layers. Invert each pan and hit sharply on the table so the layer will drop out; remove foil. Split to make 4 layers. Fill the layers and frost the top with Rum-flavored Whipped Cream. If you like, garnish with grated chocolate. Refrigerate torte at least 8 hours before serving, allowing it to mellow and become moist.

12 SERVINGS.

RUM-FLAVORED WHIPPED CREAM

In a chilled bowl, beat 2 cups chilled whipping cream, ½ cup confectioners' sugar and 2 teaspoons rum flavoring until stiff.

FRESH FRUIT COBBLER

2 cups sliced fresh peaches
  (3 or 4 medium)
1 cup sliced large red
  plums (3 or 4)
1 cup fresh blueberries
⅔ cup sugar
3 tablespoons flour
½ teaspoon cinnamon
2 tablespoons butter or
  margarine
1 cup all-purpose flour*
2 tablespoons sugar
1½ teaspoons baking powder
½ teaspoon salt
⅓ cup shortening
3 tablespoons milk
1 egg

*If using self-rising flour, omit baking powder and salt.

Heat oven to 375°. Arrange the fruits in an un-greased baking dish, 8×8×2 inches. Mix ⅔ cup sugar, 3 tablespoons flour and the cinnamon and sprinkle over the fruits. Dot with butter.

Measure 1 cup flour, 2 tablespoons sugar, the baking powder and salt into a bowl. Cut in shortening thoroughly. Mix in milk and egg. Drop the dough by spoonfuls onto the fruit. Bake 25 to 30 minutes or until golden brown. Serve warm and, if you like, with cream or ice cream.

9 SERVINGS.

DATE PUDDING

3 eggs
1 cup sugar
¼ cup all-purpose flour*
1 teaspoon baking powder
¼ teaspoon salt
2½ cups chopped dates
1 cup chopped nuts
  Whipped cream

*If using self-rising flour, decrease baking powder to ½ teaspoon.

Heat oven to 350°. Grease a baking pan, 9×9×2 inches. Beat eggs until light and fluffy. Adding sugar gradually, continue beating until the mixture is thick. Mix in flour, baking powder and salt. Stir in dates and nuts. Pour into the pan. Bake 30 minutes. Serve with whipped cream.

9 TO 12 SERVINGS.

PEACH DUMPLINGS

Pastry for 9-inch Two-crust Pie
(page 123)
6 medium peaches, peeled
and halved
¼ cup cranberry relish
2 cups brown sugar (packed)
1 cup water

Heat oven to 425°. Prepare the pastry as directed except—roll ⅔ of the dough into a 14-inch square and cut into 4 squares. Roll the remaining dough into a rectangle, 14×7 inches, and cut into 2 squares.

Place 2 peach halves on each square. Spoon cranberry relish on the peach halves. Moisten corners of squares; bring corners up to overlap and press together.

Place the dumplings in an ungreased baking dish, 11½×7½×1½ inches. Heat sugar and water to boiling and carefully pour around the dumplings. Spoon the syrup over the dumplings 2 or 3 times while baking. Bake about 40 minutes or until the crust is golden and peaches are tender. Serve warm with the syrup and, for a special occasion, top with sweetened whipped cream or light cream.

6 SERVINGS.

VARIATIONS

Company Best Apple Dumplings: Substitute 6 medium baking apples, pared and cored, for the peaches and 6 tablespoons chopped dried apricots for the cranberry relish.

Old-fashioned Apple Dumplings: Substitute 6 medium baking apples, pared and cored, for the peaches; substitute 3 tablespoons raisins and 3 tablespoons chopped nuts for the cranberry relish.

Peach Dumplings

CHERRY-BERRIES ON A CLOUD

6 egg whites
½ teaspoon cream of tartar
¼ teaspoon salt
1¾ cups sugar
2 cups chilled whipping cream
2 packages (3 ounces each)
   cream cheese, softened
1 cup sugar
1 teaspoon vanilla
2 cups miniature marshmallows
   Cherry-Berry Topping (below)

Heat oven to 275°. Butter a baking pan, 13 × 9 × 2 inches. In a large mixer bowl, beat egg whites, cream of tartar and salt until foamy. Beat in 1¾ cups sugar, 1 tablespoon at a time, and continue beating until stiff and glossy. *Do not underbeat.* Spread in the pan. Bake 1 hour. Turn off the oven; leave meringue in oven with the door closed 12 hours or longer.

In a chilled bowl, beat whipping cream until stiff. Blend cream cheese, 1 cup sugar and the vanilla. Gently fold the whipped cream and marshmallows into the cream cheese mixture; spread over the meringue. Chill 12 to 24 hours. Cut into serving pieces and top with Cherry-Berry Topping.

10 TO 12 SERVINGS.

CHERRY-BERRY TOPPING

Stir together 1 can (21 ounces) cherry pie filling, 1 teaspoon lemon juice and 2 cups sliced fresh strawberries or 1 package (16 ounces) frozen strawberries, thawed.

Is it any wonder that this show-off special never fails to wow guests? And the do-ahead feature makes it especially great for entertaining. Tangy cream cheese, whipped cream, marshmallows and the meringue base mellow together as the dessert chills.

DANISH PUFFS

½ cup butter or margarine, softened
1 cup all-purpose flour
2 tablespoons water
½ cup butter or margarine
1 cup water
1 teaspoon almond extract
1 cup all-purpose flour
3 eggs
Confectioners' Sugar Glaze (below)
Chopped nuts

Meet a close cousin of Danish pastry that has all the royal-rich family characteristics—a cream puff topping baked on a flaky pastry crust. (The topping shrinks as it cools and forms a custardy portion right in the center.)

Twinkling fast to make, Danish Puffs are so rich, in fact, that we think of them more as a dessert than a coffee cake.

Heat oven to 350°. With a pastry blender, cut ½ cup butter into 1 cup flour until the mixture looks like meal. Sprinkle 2 tablespoons water over the mixture and mix with a fork. Pat rounded teaspoonfuls (1½ level teaspoons) of the dough into 3-inch rounds on an ungreased baking sheet. The rounds should be about 3 inches apart.

For the puff topping, heat ½ cup butter and 1 cup water to a rolling boil in a saucepan. Reduce heat and quickly stir in almond extract and 1 cup flour. Stir vigorously over low heat until mixture forms a ball, about 1 minute. Remove from heat. Beat in eggs, all at one time, and continue beating until smooth.

Spread a rounded tablespoonful (1½ level tablespoons) of the batter over each round of dough, extending it just beyond the edge. (The topping will shrink slightly when it's baked.) Bake 30 minutes or until the topping is crisp. Cool; frost with the glaze and sprinkle with nuts.

2 DOZEN PUFFS.

CONFECTIONERS' SUGAR GLAZE

Mix 1½ cups confectioners' sugar, 2 tablespoons soft butter or margarine, 1½ teaspoons vanilla and 1 to 2 tablespoons warm water until smooth.

VARIATION

Danish Strips: Divide the dough in half and pat each half into a strip, 12 × 3 inches, on an ungreased baking sheet. The strips should be about 3 inches apart. Divide the batter in half and spread each half evenly over a strip. Bake about 1 hour. Cool; frost and cut into 2-inch slices.

1 cup water
½ cup butter or margarine
1 cup all-purpose flour
4 eggs
French Almond Custard
(below) or sweetened
whipped cream
Confectioners' sugar

These French-born delicacies are triple triumphs every time—surprisingly simple to make, extremely versatile and absolutely elegant.

Shape them big and round for classic cream puffs, long for chocolate éclairs, tiny for *petits choux*. Fill them with whatever strikes your fancy—like fruit, ice cream or custard for dazzling desserts. Or how about a filling of chicken, shrimp or crabmeat salad for extraordinary tea sandwiches?

Planning a party? Put Cream Puffs on the do-in-advance list. They can be made well ahead of time and refrigerated or frozen, then filled just before serving.

CREAM PUFFS

Heat oven to 400°. Heat water and butter to a rolling boil in a saucepan. Reduce heat and quickly stir in the flour. (Use a wooden spoon for easier mixing.) Stir vigorously over low heat until the mixture forms a ball, about 1 minute. Remove from heat. Beat in the eggs, all at once, and continue beating until smooth. Drop the dough by scant ¼ cupfuls 3 inches apart onto an ungreased baking sheet.

Bake 35 to 40 minutes or until puffed and golden. Cool on a wire rack. Cut off the tops and, if necessary, pull out any filaments of soft dough. Just before serving, fill puffs with French Almond Custard. Replace the tops and dust with confectioners' sugar. Refrigerate any leftover puffs.

12 PUFFS.

FRENCH ALMOND CUSTARD

½ cup sugar
½ teaspoon salt
2 tablespoons cornstarch
2 cups light cream or milk
2 egg yolks, slightly beaten
1 tablespoon butter or margarine
1 teaspoon almond extract

Mix sugar, salt and cornstarch in a saucepan. Gradually stir in light cream. Cook over medium heat, stirring constantly, until mixture thickens and boils. Boil and stir 1 minute. Remove from heat. Gradually stir about half the hot mixture into egg yolks. Blend into the hot mixture in the saucepan. Boil and stir 1 minute. Remove from heat and stir in butter and almond extract. Chill before using to fill puffs.

2 CUPS.

NAPOLEONS

1 cup butter
1½ cups all-purpose flour*
½ cup dairy sour cream
3 tablespoons granulated sugar
1 tablespoon water
1 cup confectioners' sugar
1 tablespoon milk
1 square (1 ounce) semisweet
   chocolate, melted
½ recipe French Almond Custard
   (page 152) or ½ can (18-ounce
   size) vanilla pudding

*Self-rising flour can be used in this recipe—but the baking time may be shorter.

Cut butter into flour with a pastry blender until completely mixed. (The dough will form a soft ball.) With a fork, stir in sour cream until thoroughly blended. Divide the dough in half and wrap each in plastic wrap or aluminum foil. Chill at least 8 hours.

Heat oven to 350°. Roll one half of the pastry dough on a well-floured cloth-covered board into a rectangle, 12×10 inches. Cut into 15 rectangles, each 4×2 inches. Mix granulated sugar and water and brush on the rectangles. Bake on an ungreased baking sheet 15 to 18 minutes or until light brown. Cool. Repeat with the other half of the pastry.

Mix confectioners' sugar and milk until smooth; spread on ten of the rectangles. Drizzle chocolate on the frosted rectangles. Stack 3 rectangles together with 1 tablespoon French Almond Custard between each. (A frosted rectangle should be on the top.)

10 NAPOLEONS.

JAM TARTLETS

Pastry dough for Napoleons
(above)
3 tablespoons sugar
1 tablespoon water
About ½ cup jam

Roll each half of the pastry dough 1/16 inch thick and cut into 2-inch shapes. Cut a small hole in the center of half the shapes and brush with mixture of sugar and water; place on top of the plain shapes. Fill each hole with about ½ teaspoon jam. Bake on an ungreased baking sheet 20 minutes or until light brown.

ABOUT 3½ DOZEN TARTLETS.

POTS DE CRÈME AU CHOCOLAT

1 bar (4 ounces) sweet cooking
 chocolate
2 tablespoons sugar
¾ cup light cream (20%)
2 egg yolks, slightly beaten
½ teaspoon vanilla

Heat chocolate, sugar and cream over medium heat, stirring constantly, until the chocolate is melted and mixture is smooth. Gradually beat into egg yolks, then blend in vanilla. Pour into pot de crème pots, demitasse cups or other small dessert dishes and chill. Garnish with whipped cream.

4 TO 6 SERVINGS.

BAKED RICE PUDDING

½ cup uncooked regular rice
1 cup water
½ cup sugar
1 tablespoon cornstarch
 Dash of salt
2 eggs, separated
2½ cups milk
1 tablespoon lemon juice
½ cup raisins
¼ cup sugar

Stir together rice and water in a saucepan. Heat to boiling, stirring once or twice. Reduce heat; cover and simmer 14 minutes without removing the cover or stirring. All the water should be absorbed.

Heat oven to 350°. Blend ½ cup sugar, the cornstarch and salt. Beat egg yolks slightly. Add yolks and milk to the sugar-cornstarch mixture; beat with a rotary beater. Stir in the cooked rice, lemon juice and raisins.

Pour into an ungreased 1½-quart casserole and place the casserole in a pan of very hot water (1 inch deep). Bake about 1½ hours, stirring occasionally, until the pudding is creamy and most of the liquid is absorbed. Remove from the oven, but leave the casserole in the pan of hot water.

An elegant meringue on a wholesome pudding? Why not! We think that's what makes this a something-special dessert. But if your family craves a rice pudding just like Grandma used to make, forget about the meringue. Instead, top the pudding with a hearty sprinkling of cinnamon or nutmeg and grated lemon peel. Or take a tip from one of our home-testers and serve it with lingonberry sauce.

Increase the oven temperature to 400°. Beat egg whites until foamy. Beat in ¼ cup sugar, 1 tablespoon at a time, and continue beating until stiff and glossy; spread on the pudding. Bake 8 to 10 minutes or until the meringue is golden brown. Serve warm.

6 TO 8 SERVINGS.

COMPANY CHEESECAKE

1¼ cups graham cracker crumbs (about 16 crackers)
2 tablespoons sugar
3 tablespoons butter or margarine, melted
2 packages (8 ounces each) plus 1 package (3 ounces) cream cheese, softened
1 cup sugar
2 teaspoons grated lemon peel
¼ teaspoon vanilla
3 eggs
1 cup dairy sour cream, Cherry Glaze (below) or Strawberry Glaze (below)

Heat oven to 350°. Mix cracker crumbs, 2 tablespoons sugar and the butter. Press the crumb mixture firmly and evenly in the bottom of a 9-inch springform pan. Bake 10 minutes. Cool.

Reduce the oven temperature to 300°. Beat cream cheese in a large mixer bowl. Gradually add 1 cup sugar, beating until fluffy. Add lemon peel and vanilla. Then beat in eggs, one at a time. Pour over the crumb mixture.

Bake 1 hour or until the center is firm. Cool to room temperature. Spread with sour cream or one of the glazes. Chill at least 3 hours. Before serving, loosen edge of cheesecake with knife and remove the side of the pan.

12 SERVINGS.

CHERRY GLAZE

Drain 1 can (16 ounces) pitted red tart cherries, reserving liquid. Add enough water to the reserved cherry liquid to measure 1 cup. Mix ½ cup sugar and 2 tablespoons cornstarch in a small saucepan; stir in the 1 cup cherry liquid. Cook, stirring constantly, until the mixture thickens and boils. Boil and stir 1 minute. Remove from heat. Stir in the cherries and a few drops of red food color. Cool thoroughly.

STRAWBERRY GLAZE

Mash enough fresh strawberries to measure 1 cup. Mix 1 cup sugar and 3 tablespoons cornstarch in a small saucepan. Stir in ⅓ cup water and the strawberries. Cook, stirring constantly, until the mixture thickens and boils. Boil and stir 1 minute. Cool thoroughly.

Steamed Plum Pudding

STEAMED PLUM PUDDING

1 cup milk
3 cups soft bread crumbs
½ cup shortening, melted
½ cup molasses
1 cup all-purpose flour*
1 teaspoon soda
1 teaspoon salt
2 teaspoons cinnamon
¼ teaspoon allspice
¼ teaspoon cloves
½ cup cut-up raisins
½ cup finely cut-up citron
   Amber Sauce (below) or
   Sherried Hard Sauce (below)

*If using self-rising flour, decrease soda to ½ teaspoon and omit salt.

Generously grease a 4-cup mold. In a large bowl, pour milk over bread crumbs and mix in shortening and molasses. Stir in remaining ingredients except the sauce. Pour into the mold and cover tightly with aluminum foil.

Place a rack in a Dutch oven about 1 or 2 inches from the bottom. (If the rack is not adjustable, simply balance it on 2 inverted custard cups.) Pour in boiling water up to the level of the rack and place the filled mold on rack. Heat to boiling. Cover and keep water boiling over low heat 3 hours or until a wooden pick inserted in center of pudding comes out clean. (If more water is needed during the steaming period, lift lid and quickly add boiling water.) Unmold the pudding and cut into slices. Serve warm with one of the sauces.

6 TO 8 SERVINGS.

The original English "Christmas pudding"—a holiday tradition that dates back to the 1700's—usually included raisins, which at the time were called plums. Thus the dessert came to be called "Plum Pudding."

For this up-to-date version, we ignited warm brandy and then poured it over the pudding. Another method calls for soaking small sugar cubes in lemon extract and placing them around the unmolded pudding. Light just one cube, then stand back and watch the flames encircle the pudding. Whichever method you use, one thing is sure: For the ultimate in drama, out with the lights.

Serve this time-honored dessert with an old Yorkshire adage: "In as many homes as you eat plum pudding in the 12 days following Christmas, so many happy months will you have during the year."

AMBER SAUCE

1 cup brown sugar (packed) or
   granulated sugar
½ cup light corn syrup
¼ cup butter or margarine
½ cup half-and-half

Mix all ingredients in a small saucepan. Cook over low heat 5 minutes, stirring occasionally. Serve warm.

2 CUPS.

SHERRIED HARD SAUCE

In a small mixer bowl, beat ½ cup soft butter on high speed until very creamy, fluffy and light in color—about 5 minutes. Gradually beat in 1 cup confectioners' sugar until smooth. Blend in 1 tablespoon sherry or brandy. Chill about 1 hour.

1 CUP.